THE PAN-AFRICANISTS

Ife
Bronze

THE PAN-AFRICANISTS

Paintings by
Barrington Watson

with a foreword by
Kofi Annan

Africa World Press, Inc.

P.O. Box 1892  P.O. Box 48
Trenton, NJ 08607 Asmara, ERITREA

Africa World Press, Inc.

P.O. Box 1892
Trenton, NJ 08607

P.O. Box 48
Asmara, ERITREA

Copyright: © 2000 Ian Randle Publishers

First North American Edition by Africa World Press, Inc. 2000

Library of Congress Cataloging-in-Publication Data

Watson, Barrington, 1931-
    The pan-Africanists / paintings by Barrington Watson; with a foreword by Kofi Annan.
    p. cm.
    ISBN 0-86543-809-9 — ISBN 0-86543-810-2 (pbk.)
    1. Pan-Africanism. 2. Afro-Americans –Biography. 3. Africans - Biography.
    4. Afro-Americans – Portraits. 5. Africans – Portraits. I. Title.
    DT18.W37 2000
    920'009296073   dc2199-055236

Contents

Foreword by the Secretary-General

I am pleased to introduce this remarkable collection of paintings and biographies of seventeen Pan-African leaders. Ranging from Frederick Douglass to Rosa Parks, from Martin Luther King to Nelson Mandela, from W.E.B. DuBois to Marcus Garvey, this extraordinary book reveals in image and word the contribution of these men and women to the lives of all people of African descent.

While all these leaders would have continued to struggle for Africa's future, I believe they would have been prouder still of the efforts made by Africans today to lift their continent out of poverty and conflict and into a better future. They would have seen that beyond the Africa of deadly warfare and endemic poverty, there is an Africa that is rejecting the dogmas of the past and embracing pragmatic progress under the rule of law; an Africa that – in a growing number of cases – is making a genuine effort to reject violence, embrace democracy, endorse human rights and promote economic reform.

The Pan-Africanist leaders honoured in this book sought to advance freedom and promote equality, but did so at different times and under different conditions. In the United States, Douglass and Harriet Tubman struggled to end slavery, while Martin Luther King and Rosa Parks showed the world how the courage of an individual can transform a nation. In Africa, Lumumba, Kenyatta and Nkrumah all led liberation movements to make Africa free.

Finally, in our time, Nelson Mandela defeated apartheid in South Africa, and in so doing, won a victory for all mankind. But as with his distinguished fellow Pan-African leaders, Mandela knew that it would not be enough to defeat the evil of discrimination. He knew that something new had to be created as well, a political, social and economic order in which all Africans, regardless of race, could prosper and contribute to the future of their nation.

The path of peace, reconciliation and equality that Mandela forged for the people of South Africa is a model for every nation, and all peoples. The principles and values at the heart of his struggle are universal: human rights, co-existence, democracy and development. By bringing these principles to life in South Africa, he honoured the struggle of all Pan-Africans and advanced the cause of the United Nations.

In the next century, a new generation of men and women of African descent must carry the struggle further still, into a new era when the hopes and aspirations of their leaders will be realized, once and for all.

Kofi A. Annan

Introduction: Pan-Africanism

Modern pan-Africanism is about one hundred years old. It was in July 1900 that Henry Sylvester Williams, a Trinidad-born barrister, organized the first pan-African conference in London. He wanted, he stated, to 'bring into closer touch with each other the peoples of African descent throughout the world.' This first gathering was a small affair – only four representatives from Africa itself attended – but it was the beginning of a movement that would grow in the course of the century, attracting men and women around the world to an ideal of justice and human rights.

Pan-Africanism is a people's movement, a struggle against the unjust and unlawful oppression of Black people. Such oppression is nothing new, for its origins lie in the enslavement and exploitation of Black people dating from the first appearance of Europeans in Africa. From the beginning of the sixteenth century to the end of the nineteenth, slavery and the slave trade devastated vast areas of the continent. Some fifteen millions were shipped across the Atlantic to the plantations of the Americas, ranging from Brazil to the southern states of the US.

This massive and violent transplantation of peoples damaged Africa's development, encouraging conflict and emptying parts of the continent of its youngest and fittest people. It also created large Black communities on the other side of the Atlantic, in almost every Caribbean island, in many South American countries and in the American South. Oppressed and exploited as slaves, these people survived the horrors of the plantation and kept alive important elements of their African culture through the generations. With the abolition of slavery in the nineteenth century came social reforms and the hope of a better life, but racism and discrimination persisted. Migration spread the African diaspora more widely; Black people moved to Europe, to the northern states of the US and Canada.

The development of Black communities around the world coincided with a new phase in Europe's penetration of Africa. Just 16 years before the first pan-African conference, the major European powers had gathered in Berlin to discuss the sharing out of colonies in Africa. In what was known as the 'scramble for Africa' the British, French, German and other governments carved up the continent, sending in troops, settlers and missionaries to almost every territory that was not already occupied.

The heyday of colonialism involved the wide-scale exploitation of African resources and African people. It also reinforced European ideas of white superiority and Black inferiority, ideas that had been used to justify the inhuman practice of slavery. The achievements of Black people and African cultures were dismissed as 'primitive'. Many of the colonialists saw it as their duty to impose European beliefs and systems on the colonized peoples – whether they wanted them or not.

From this experience of oppression and humiliation emerged a new generation of African leaders, mostly educated in European-run schools but eager to rid their countries of the colonial masters. Such leaders dreamed of seeing their nations free of outside rule and of restoring a sense of pride in their people's African identity. Some also had an even greater dream – of seeing a divided and exploited Africa reunited.

The coming together of the new African leaders and the Black communities outside the continent marks the beginning of modern pan-Africanism. The struggle of the emerging African nations against European colonialism resonated with the experiences of Black people across the world, who had long been faced with discrimination and violence. This shared understanding of the need for freedom and justice became inseparable from the issue of Africa and 'Africanness'. Just as those opposed to colonialism in the continent proclaimed an independent Africa, so those whose ancestors had been removed from there as slaves looked towards Africa as the source of their culture and identity.

The movement known as pan-Africanism can hence be partly defined as 'the backlash against slavery', an expression of resistance by people whose present-day reality is the direct consequence of a history of slavery. From the ghettoes of New York or Detroit to the rural communities of the Caribbean, individuals and groups have turned their gaze towards Africa as their true homeland, as the place to which they truly belong. It can also be defined as a series of aspirations arising from Africa itself and from its various nations and peoples. Aspirations which include the desire for peace and freedom, an end to foreign exploitation, unity and solidarity between Africans.

Pan-Africanism can perhaps be best described through some of its strongest features:

– It is an association or a movement, aimed at giving Black people full participation in the political, social, cultural and economic dimensions of world affairs.

– It is unmistakably and emphatically Afrocentric, that is to say it takes Africa as its starting point for all its ideas and beliefs.

– It assumes that all Black people around the world constitute a single family, descended from a common African origin.

– It stands for the decolonization of Africa and the independence of all states. It is totally opposed to any form of racial injustice or discrimination.

– It is committed to the universal recognition of the full dignity of Black people and their equality as citizens of the world.

As well as proclaiming these central principles, pan-Africanism insists on a rewriting of history to give to Black people their rightful place both in the past and the present. One of the movement's founding fathers, W.E.B. Dubois, explained this goal:

"Pan-Africa will seek to preserve its own past history, and write the present, erasing from its literature the lies and distortions about black folks which have disgraced the last centuries of European and American literature; . . . pan-Africa seeks the end of making Africans not simply profitable workers for industry nor stool pigeons for propaganda, but making them modern, intelligent, responsible men [and women] of vision and character."

This history is explored in the lives of the seventeen men and women that follow. Not all of them necessarily belonged formally to a panafricanist organization or even used the term in descriptions of themselves. The life of each one of them, though, manifests the core values of pan-Africanism as described above. Together their lives represent a powerful embodiment of the history of this social movement.

Of course, it goes much further back in time, to the earliest known civilizations of ancient Egypt, when more than 5,000 years ago Black people were instrumental in forming one of the most impressive and durable cultures of any time. Millenia later from 700 to 1500 AD, the Ghana, Mali and Songhay Empires of Western Africa were engaged in sophisticated trade and cultural links, when most of Europe was living through endless wars, epidemics and barbarity. Little of this history appears in the Euro-centric accounts that have been imposed on colonized peoples over the centuries.

The immediate precursor of pan-Africanism, however, were the abolitionist struggles of the nineteenth century and the culture of resistance that grew up around slavery in the Americas. Figures such as Harriet Tubman and Frederick Douglass were vitally important in undermining the institution of slavery by encouraging slaves to escape and by galvanizing opposition to the system among other Americans and overseas. In every territory where slavery existed, slaves were also instrumental in securing their own freedom — by escape, revolt, or in the case of Haiti, full-scale revolution. In the course of these struggles, the image of a distant Africa was never far from the minds of those who saw themselves as imprisoned in an alien country.

When the slaves were eventually freed, there were some who returned to Africa from the US or the Caribbean. Individuals such as James Holy Johnson, Edward Wilmot Blyden and Henry Highland Garnet visited or stayed in West Africa, establishing schools, churches and hospitals in Liberia and Sierra Leone, the two countries settled by freed slaves. Others stayed in the US and the Caribbean, undergoing the trials and tribulations which followed emancipation. Individuals such as Dubois, who was born in the immediate aftermath of abolition, had to struggle against institutional racism to become leading thinkers and spokesmen for Black people and their rights.

In the first two decades of the twentieth century, the figure of Jamaican-born Marcus Garvey loomed large in the development of pan-African thinking. With his 'Back to Africa' slogan, Garvey inspired millions of followers in his United Negro Improvement Association to take pride in their African heritage and to contest the notion of white domination.

If the birth of modern pan-Africanism can be traced to the 1900 conference, its evolution can also be followed through a series of succeeding conferences and meetings. From the first gathering in London, four more pan-African conferences took place between 1919 and 1945, all of them inspired and organized by the influential figure of Dubois. Of these perhaps the most important was the fifth, held in Manchester in 1945 and attended by almost 100 delegates from Africa, Europe and the Americas. Among those present were George Padmore, another Trinidadian who devoted his life to the cause of bringing African and African-descended people together with the common purpose of ending colonialism. C.L.R. James, one of the greatest historians of the twentieth century and a life-long enemy of colonialism, took part. Also there were Jomo Kenyatta and Kwame Nkrumah, later to be the leaders of independent Kenya and Ghana respectively.

The 1945 conference showed how far pan-Africanism had come. While earlier conferences had issued polite appeals to European governments for better conditions in the colonies, the meeting which followed the end of the Second World War was altogether more militant. Inspired by the defeat of Fascism and particularly by the return to power in Ethiopia of Emperor Haile Selassie I, the delegates called for an end to all colonial interference in Africa. As Sid Lamelle, a historian of pan-Africanism, puts it: 'Pan-Africanism was no longer simply a protest movement by people of African descent in the Caribbean and the United States; it was becoming a weapon with which African nationalists would fight colonial rule.'

The protest movement in the US, meanwhile, was gathering impetus with the fight against segregation in states such as Alabama. Here, figures such as Martin Luther King, Jr. and Rosa Parks led the way in dismantling

racist laws which sought to separate Blacks from whites in all areas of life. They were preceded by the charismatic Paul Robeson, who never renounced his Marxist faith throughout the Cold War and who saw socialism as the only road to Black freedom. Later opponents of racism in the US included the unique Muhammad Ali, whose political integrity cost him three years of his boxing career, and the mercurial Malcolm X, who emerged from a life of crime to be the most outspoken Black Muslim of his generation.

As decolonization became a reality, pan-Africanists such as Nkrumah and Kenyatta found themselves in power. They were joined by Julius Nyerere in 1962, who created a united Tanzania and tried to introduce an original form of rural socialism. Elsewhere, however, the transition from colonial rule proved more traumatic, as in the Congo, where Belgium and the US conspired to bring about the downfall of the radical Patrice Lumumba in 1961.

Post-independence Africa has had more than its fair share of pain – civil wars, continued foreign interference, droughts and famines. Yet among the bad news certain positive developments are often overlooked. One of these has been the survival of the pan-African ideal and its practical implementation in the struggle against apartheid and racism in Southern Africa. From its founding in 1963 in Addis Ababa, the Organization of African Unity played a leading role in the campaign against the white-dominated regimes in South Africa and Zimbabwe (then Rhodesia). The dismantling of apartheid and the emergence of a free Zimbabwe owe much to the efforts of leaders such as Nkrumah and Nyerere. When Nelson Mandela finally walked free in 1990 after almost three decades in prison, it was a moment of victory not just for Black South Africans, but for pan-Africanists everywhere.

A century after a group of Black activists first met in London, the world has changed beyond recognition. Institutional racism has been largely demolished; colonialism is a thing of the past (although neo-colonialism is alive and well, not least in the shape of Africa's crippling debt crisis). But the ideals of pan-Africanism are no less relevant today than they were then. The dream of a united Africa is still unrealized, while Black people around the world continue to be treated all too often as second-class citizens. While disunity and discrimination remain obstacles to a fairer global community, the pan-African vision of cooperation and justice will inspire and mobilize future generations around the world.

THE PAN-AFRICANISTS

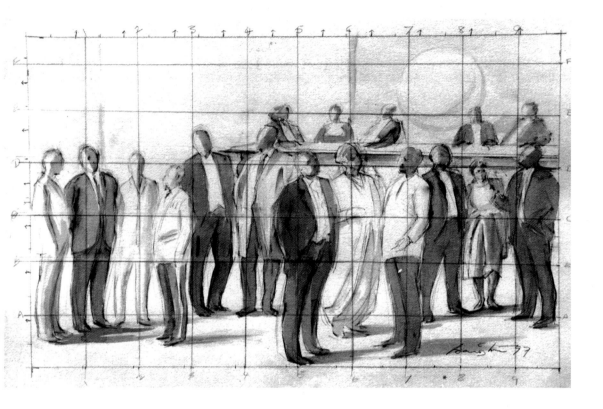

16   *Frederick Douglass*

Frederick Douglass

1817-1895

One of the most prominent activists against American slavery, Frederick Douglass was an exceptional and inspiring orator. Not only did he himself escape from slavery, but he encouraged other Blacks in the southern states to do the same both before and during the American Civil War. He went on to become one of the most important Afro-American leaders in the 19th century.

Frederick Augustus Washington Bailey was born a slave in Tuckahoe, Maryland. The son of a black slave mother, Harriet Bailey, and a white man, he managed to teach himself to read and write, but was mostly forced to work long hours for his master. When he dared to teach at a Sunday school, he was flogged. Such degrading experiences filled him with a deep hatred of slavery and he tried to escape to the freedom of the northern states in 1836. A second attempt succeeded in 1838, when he reached Massachusetts. Here, with forged papers, he adopted the new name of Frederick Douglass.

It was in Nantucket, Massachusetts that Douglass' gifts as a public speaker were first discovered. At an anti-slavery meeting in 1841 he got to his feet and spoke movingly of his own experiences. He was soon employed as an agent of the Massachusetts Anti-Slavery Society, speaking at many meetings and working with the Underground Railroad – a secret network that helped slaves to escape to the north. He was once described as 'a recent graduate from the institution of slavery with his diploma on his back.' Because of his direct experience of slavery's degradation, Douglass was able to speak with extraordinary passion and authority. He described how slaves were routinely flogged for 'impudence'. 'A young slave must accompany his overseer or master with hat in hand', he said, 'and woe betide him if he fails to acknowledge a favour of any sort with a "tankee master".'

A handsome giant of a man, he was able to keep his audiences spellbound with his unusual eloquence. Indeed, so eloquent was Douglass that some opponents of the anti-slavery movement claimed that he could not have been a slave at all and was an impostor, used by the abolitionists for propaganda purposes. Douglass' fame as an orator rapidly spread, and soon he was attracting very large crowds to his public meetings.

In 1845 Douglass travelled to England, partly to win support for his cause and partly to avoid the risk of being recaptured under the

Fugitive Slave Laws. Sympathizers raised enough money to purchase his legal freedom, and he spoke to huge audiences throughout the country. He also had meetings with influential politicians and campaigners who were pressing for an end to slavery in the US. At the end of his tour of England and Ireland, he returned to the US in 1847, telling a capacity crowd in London before he left: 'I will go back for the sake of my brethren, to suffer with them, to toil with them and to endure insult with them.'

Once back in the US, Douglass started up an abolitionist newspaper, *North Star*, and continued working with the Underground Railroad, to such an extent that he became known as its 'station-master and conductor'. In the meantime, his dramatic account of his life as a slave, *Narrative of the Life of Frederick Douglass, an American Slave* (1845) had been published and had caused enormous controversy. During the 1850s he was a friend and associate of another famous abolitionist, John Brown, who believed that slavery could only be destroyed by an armed uprising of slaves and their supporters. Douglass disagreed with this strategy and refused to be involved with the seizure of arms at Harpers Ferry, which led to Brown's arrest and execution. Even so, when the plot was discovered, Douglass was forced to flee for his life, finding sanctuary in Europe.

By this time, hostility was growing in the US between the cotton-growing states of the South (where slaves had been used since the 17th century) and the industrial North. Abraham Lincoln was a candidate in the 1860 presidential election and had pledged to abolish slavery, so Douglass returned to campaign on his behalf. Shortly after Lincoln won, the southern states decided to break away from the Union and American Civil War broke out in 1861 between the pro-slavery Confederates of the south and the abolitionist Federal government in Washington DC. Douglass threw himself into the struggle and was asked by President Lincoln to help mobilize Black troops on the Federal side. He raised two regiments, the Massachusetts 54th and 55th, which gained a reputation for outstanding bravery in the course of the war. Fighting against the discrimination faced by Black troops, he forced Lincoln to improve his regiments' conditions, issuing his famous call 'Men of Color, To Arms!'

Eventually in 1865 the Federal forces were victorious and slavery was officially abolished in the entire US. In the aftermath of the war, the US constitution was amended to include this act of abolition, and Douglass was personally responsible for the enactment of the 13th, 14th and 15th Amendments.

After the war, Douglass was appointed to a series of official positions: US Marshal for the District of Columbia (1877-1881), recorder of deeds for the District of Columbia (1881-1886) and US minister to Haiti (1889-1891). In all these posts he spoke out for the rights of minorities and oppressed people. As US representative in Haiti, he had the difficult task of speaking on behalf of a superpower that had long been hostile to the existence and independence of the first black republic in the Americas. Nevertheless, he was greatly respected by the Haitian government and people, who saw him as a natural ally.

In later years Douglass worked on his memoirs, revising *Narrative of the Life of Frederick Douglass* into a new account of his life as a slave. This was called *Life and Times of Frederick Douglass* and appeared in 1882.

Frederick Douglass died in Washington DC on 20 February 1895.

Douglass is best remembered as a passionate critic of slavery and an early advocate of human rights and equality. His greatest weapon was his command of language, which enabled him to speak and write with great conviction and persuasiveness. He was once asked to speak at a meeting to commemorate America's 4th of July Independence Day:

"What to the American slave is your 4th of July? I answer a day that reveals to him more than all other days in the year, the gross injustice and cruelty to which he is the constant victim. To him your celebration is a sham, your boasted liberty an unholy license, your national greatness swelling vanity . . . your sermons and thanksgivings with all your religious parades and solemnity are to him bombast, fraud, deception, impiety and hypocrisy – a thin veil to cover up crimes which would disgrace a nation of savages. "

Above all, he was a living symbol of freedom and Black self-advancement, not just among the Black community, but in the US as a whole.

DID YOU KNOW? Douglass was the first Afro-American to be nominated as candidate for Vice-President in a US election in 1872. The small Labor Reform Party chose him as their candidate, but he never stood.

READ MORE: Frederick Douglass, *Narrative of the Life of Frederick Douglass* (New York: Anchor)

Harriet Tubman

1820?-1913

Born a slave in Bucktown, Dorchester County, Maryland, Harriet Tubman's real name was Araminta Ross, but at an early age people began to call her by her mother's name, Harriet. Her precise date of birth is not known, but was somewhere between 1816 and 1823. She was one of eleven children, born to Harriet Greene and Benjamin Ross, both slaves. She endured a harsh childhood, later saying: 'I grew up like a neglected weed – ignorant of liberty having no experience of it'. From the age of five she worked as a domestic servant, and by twelve she was working in the fields of the plantation. Her owner often contracted her out to other plantation owners, and she was always forced to work long hours in the fields. But at home, life was more bearable. Her father taught her valuable knowledge at an early age about surviving in the woods – this would come in useful later in her life.

When Harriet was thirteen, a terrible incident left her scarred for life. A plantation supervisor was about to beat another slave, and she intervened. The supervisor hit her with a two-pound weight, fracturing her skull. For the rest of her life she suffered from blackouts resulting from this incident, although she managed to regain her physical strength. In 1844 she married John Tubman, a freed slave, although it is said that she loved him much more than he loved her.

Her life changed further when she and other slaves on the plantation were handed over to the legal guardian of the master, who was too young to run the plantation after his father died. On learning that the guardian intended to sell the slaves wherever he could, Harriet decided to make a break for freedom, leaving behind her husband who refused to accompany her. She made it to the state of Pennsylvania, where slavery was illegal, in 1849, finding work as a washerwoman in Philadelphia. Even though she had escaped from Maryland, she still had to be careful as in 1850 the Fugitive Slave Laws were passed in order to allow slave owners to recapture their human 'property'.

After two years in Pennsylvania, Harriet Tubman was confident enough to help other slaves to escape. She had devised the idea that she could lead her Black brothers and sisters out of slavery by guiding them across state lines. She had said that she felt like she was in heaven in what was called 'free soil' and wanted others to experience the same sense of freedom. Her first mission took her to Baltimore in Maryland, where she made contact with one of

her sisters, Mary Ann Bowley, and two children, whom she led to freedom. When she went to look for her husband, however, she found that he had already remarried.

Soon afterwards, Harriet became involved in the Underground Railroad, the network of routes that helped slaves to escape to such free states as Philadelphia, Ohio and Indiana as well as Canada. This was no railway, but rather a system of individuals who assisted the slaves by guiding them by night and hiding them during the day. Railway terms were used as code words – the places where the fugitives hid were termed 'stations', the slaves themselves were 'passengers' or 'merchandise', while those who helped transport the runaways were called 'conductors'.

The centre of the network was southern Pennsylvania, from where the runaways usually made their way through New England to Quebec. From 1830 to about 1860, the Underground Railroad was responsible for the escape of some 100,000 slaves, many of them reaching Canada or free northern states of the US.

Many whites as well as Blacks were active in helping the fugitive slaves reach safety. Some were Quakers and other Christians, but all were abolitionists, believing that slavery must end in the US. The success of the Underground Railroad infuriated many Southerners, particularly the slave-owners, and it increased the tension between North and South that was to lead to the American Civil War.

Harriet became famous for her fearless participation in the Underground Railroad's activities. She personally led 18 expeditions into the slaving states, personally guiding at least 300 people to safety in Canada. A legend soon grew up around her, and she was popularly known as 'Moses' for her role in leading

her people to safety. A deeply religious woman, she believed that she was always watched over by a guardian angel. Although there was a $40,000 reward on her head, Harriet was never captured and was proud that she never lost a single slave on her many expeditions. One such mission took place in December 1854, when she led three of her brothers and three other slaves northwards by night through forests and across rivers to Philadelphia and then on to Canada. On another occasion, she rescued her aged parents.

On each expedition, Harriet would lead the group at night and then, during the day, when the others were safely hidden, she would scout the area ahead, looking for food and assistance. Sometimes, she discovered an unexpected obstacle or danger and had to plan a change in their route.

Harriet Tubman could neither read nor write, but she was famous for her sayings and her grim sense of humour. 'Lord, you have been with me through six troubles. Be with me on the seventh', she said often, as well as her claim that 'I nebber run my train off de track and I nebber lost a passenger.'

During her brave work for the Railroad, Harriet met and became an associate of other prominent abolitionists such as Frederick Douglass, William H. Seward and the ill-fated John Brown. But perhaps because she was a woman, or perhaps because she was illiterate, she never achieved in her lifetime the recognition that other anti-slavery activists enjoyed. Even so, William Still, one of the Underground Railroad's most respected leaders, said of her that she was a woman who knew no fear and was one of the bravest women ever to live.

When the American Civil War broke out in 1861, Harriet Tubman naturally took the side of the Union government and was enrolled as a nurse for three years, tending to the sick and wounded in the Carolinas and in Florida. She was also used as a scout and a spy. Contemporary reports remember her as a distinctive figure, wearing a bandanna on her head and with many missing teeth. She even led a corps of local Black soldiers in the Second Carolina Volunteers in several raids, collecting valuable information. General Saxon said that 'she made many a raid inside the enemy lines, displaying remarkable courage, zeal and fidelity'. Even so, Harriet was not generously rewarded, being paid only $200 for the work she did over the three years and making a living by selling chickens, pies and root beer.

Harriet lived into her nineties, continuing to raise money for Black schools in Auburn, New York, where from 1908 she also maintained a retirement home for elderly Black people. She remained famous for her involvement in the abolitionist movement during her long life, but it was only later, with the growth of the Black civil rights movement, that her unique contribution was fully recognized.

DID YOU KNOW? Utterly ruthless when it came to the success of her expeditions, Harriet Tubman carried a pistol on her freedom raids and was heard to offer those who had second thoughts about escaping a choice : 'You'll be free or die!'

READ MORE: Ann Petry, *Harriet Tubman: Conductor on the Underground Railroad* (New York: Harper Trophy)

W.E.B. Dubois

1868-1963

William Edward Burghardt Dubois was a trailblazer in every sense. The first Black American to receive a doctoral degree, he became a distinguished scholar and highly influential writer, as well as one of the most important founders of the pan-Africanist movement.

Born on 23 February 1868 to Mary Silvina and Alfred Dubois in the small but relatively prosperous Black community in Great Barrington, Massachusetts, the young Dubois was an industrious student, and his work was already published in the local newspaper at the age of fourteen. He graduated from high school early and went to Fisk University. From there he won a scholarship to the University of Berlin and then went on to Harvard, where he obtained his doctorate. His thesis, which was subsequently published, was a brilliant analysis of the African slave trade to the US and its eventual suppression.

Dubois was now determined to build an academic career, and from 1894 to 1896 he worked as Professor of Greek and Latin at Wilberforce University, Ohio, before teaching sociology at the University of Pennsylvania. During this time he carried out research for what was one of his many classic academic works, *Philadelphia Negro* (1899). In 1897, Dubois took a professorship at Atlanta University, where he taught economics and history until 1910. He was chairman of the sociology department there from 1934 to 1944. In 1903 the book *The Souls of Black Folk* was published, which warned prophetically that violence would be the result of segregation policies in the US. Writing of Black spirituals – later to be made internationally popular by Paul Robeson – Dubois described them as 'the music of an unhappy people, of the children of disappointment; they tell of death and suffering and unvoiced longing toward a truer world.' This book is said to have had a significant influence on Marcus Garvey, who was only sixteen when it was first published.

But Dubois's long life was not merely filled with academic achievements (although these in themselves were remarkable for any Black man in an age when prejudice, segregation and even lynchings were rife). His study of American society, the slave trade and Black history had led him to become an activist in the cause of pan-African unity and he devoted enormous energy to the founding and development of pan-African organizations. In July 1900 the historic First Pan-African Congress took place

in London, called by the Trinidadian barrister Henry Sylvester Williams and attended by 32 delegates from African nations and the Americas. Designed to 'bring into closer touch with each other the peoples of African descent throughout the world', the Congress was addressed by Dubois, whose message was sent to governments around the world: 'Let the black subjects of all Nations take courage, strive ceaselessly, and fight bravely, that they may prove to the world their incontestable right to be counted among the great brotherhood of mankind.'

Dubois was actively involved in subsequent congresses in the 1920s, which became more influential and better attended as his reputation among Black activists worldwide increased. In 1921, for instance, the Third Pan-African Congress attracted 41 delegates from Africa, 24 Africans living in Europe and seven delegates from the Caribbean. This Congress condemned imperialist atrocities in the Congo and affirmed racial equality to be 'the founding stone of world and human advancement'.

In 1905 Dubois and other pioneering Black American leaders met to debate strategy over civil rights. Out of this gathering emerged the National Association for the Advancement of Colored People (NAACP), which was launched in 1910. A founding member of the NAACP, Dubois also edited its journal, *Crisis*, which began publication the same year. This early and highly influential magazine was the first document to attract my attention when, at the age of seven or eight, I sat on my father's knee and plagued him with questions about the many pictures of Black people in the journal. I recall my father explaining that one such person was a famous inventor, Dr Carver,

responsible for, among other things, the creation of peanut butter. This achievement alone elevated Dr Carver to great heights in my mind.

The NAACP was extremely effective in galvanizing Black and white liberal opinion in the US against segregation and institutional racism. Its membership included such luminaries as Whitney Young and Martin Luther King Jr., and it was instrumental in desegregating schools in the US. But there were inevitably disagreements within the organization and with other Black leaders such as Booker T. Washington over how best to achieve radical reforms in the US. In 1934, Dubois left the NAACP, returning to rejoin the organization ten years later.

By this time, Dubois had become attracted to Marxist theory as a way of explaining what he called 'the twentieth century's problem of the color line'. In a book entitled *Black Folk, Then and Now*, he suggested that the only solution to racism and imperialism around the world was the mass revolutionary uprising of people of African descent. He remained acutely aware of the cultural ambiguity surrounding Black Americans and wrote of this identity problem in *Dusk of Dawn*:

'Africa is of course my fatherland. Yet neither my father nor my father's father ever saw Africa or cared over-much for it. My mother's folk were closer and yet their direct connection, in culture and race, became tenuous; still, my tie to Africa is strong. On this vast continent were born and lived a large portion of my direct ancestors going back a thousand years or more.'

Joseph Casely Hayford, an influential leader in Sierra Leone, perceptively observed of Dubois: 'One even feels his twinness, An

American, a Negro, twin souls, two thoughts, two unreconciled strivings.'

Dubois's return to the NAACP as Director of Special Research in 1944 was marked by controversy and disagreements. The US government was by now openly hostile to the organization, and in 1951 Dubois found himself indicted under the McCarran Act for having called on the United Nations to condemn the American government for human rights abuses. He was eventually cleared of the charges made against him. Confirmed in his belief that socialism and Black emancipation were interlinked, he joined the Communist Party in 1961 and that same year left the US. In his later years, he had become increasingly saddened by what he saw as the intolerance of his own government towards his ideas. A brief stay in the Soviet Union disillusioned him still further, and he emigrated to Ghana, under President Nkrumah, where he became a citizen and remained until his death in 1963. He had a state funeral, but significantly the US government sent nobody to pay tribute. His home is now owned by the government, and it is there that he is buried. Known as the Dubois Centre, it has a good library dedicated to Black history where I have spent many hours of useful research.

It was always a pleasure to converse with Dr Dubois, when I knew him as an old man. He inspired all who heard him to follow in his path, a path made easier for succeeding generations by pioneers such as him. When he spoke of history, he made it come alive in a way that few can achieve. He was fittingly christened the 'father of pan-Africa' by George Padmore.

DID YOU KNOW? Such was the climate of racism at the beginning of the twentieth century that Dubois was not allowed to stay on the segregated campus at the University of Pennsylvania, even though he taught classes there.

READ MORE: Eric J. Sundquist, *The Oxford W.E.B. Dubois Reader* (New York: Oxford University Press)

28   *Marcus Garvey*

Marcus Garvey

1887-1940

Marcus Mosiah Garvey probably had more worldwide impact than any other person from the Caribbean in the 20th century. He was an inspirational leader, the founder of an organization with two million members across forty countries, and one of the first and greatest pan-Africanists.

Born in the rural seaside town of St Ann's Bay, Jamaica, the last of eleven children, he grew up in a poor family, his father working as a stone mason, his mother baking and selling cakes. His parents were devout Christians and encouraged an appetite for reading in their children. Until the age of twelve, he had little idea of the significance of race and colour, as he grew up in a small community where a few white families mixed easily enough with the Black majority. But then it was made clear to him that his early white friends were to be separated and sent to a different – and better – school, away from 'niggers' like him.

Leaving school at 14, he became a printer's apprentice before working as a printer in Kingston, where he led a strike for higher wages. It is said that he carried a dictionary in his pocket, aiming to learn five new words every day. He had written pamphlets and developed his political ideas before he left to travel around South and Central America in 1910. He later said that his first-hand experience of conditions on banana plantations in Panama and Costa Rica opened his eyes to the oppression suffered by Black people in the Americas. At that time, there was a huge amount of emigration from the English-speaking Caribbean islands to places such as Cuba and Panama, where work was more freely available in the sugar plantations or in constructing the Panama Canal. The workers who left islands like Jamaica and Barbados often faced poor conditions and racism, and many died in Panama from epidemics of yellow fever and malaria.

There were several important influences on the young Garvey. His own experience had shown him that colonial Jamaica's education system was weighted against Black children and removed all but the 'official' version of history from its textbooks. Jamaica's tradition of popular struggle, exemplified by the Maroons and the figures of Paul Bogle and George William Gordon, was not taught in the classroom, but it nevertheless lived on among the people as their unwritten history. Such ideas were strengthened in Garvey by Dr Robert Love, a Bahamian living in Jamaica who was an outspoken nationalist and critic of the colonial system. Deeply unpopular with the white authorities, Dr Love managed to win an election to the Kingston City Council in 1898, from where he spoke often of women's rights and the need to extend education to the poorest members of society. At the same time, Black intellectuals such as W.E. Dubois, Booker T. Washington and the Trinidadian lawyer Sylvester Williams began to spread their ideas on Black emancipation throughout the region. These influences merged with Garvey's own direct understanding of colonial oppression.

When Garvey returned to Jamaica in 1914, after a two-year stay in Britain, he founded the Universal Negro Improvement Association (UNIA). The aim of this organization was to campaign for equal rights and economic independence for black people and to create a united Africa to which they might one day return. Garvey believed that all black people, whether in the Caribbean, North America or Africa itself, formed one nation which had been broken up by European imperialism and which should be reunified. Garvey's slogan was 'Up! Up! you mighty people, you can accomplish what you will.'

In 1916 Garvey left for the US, where he built up support for the UNIA and created a newspaper, *The Negro World*. His influence was strongest in New York, Detroit and Philadelphia, but there were branches in Europe, Latin America and every Caribbean island. The UNIA ran a network of centres called Liberty Halls, which offered social services to black communities. It also supported a chain of black-run small businesses. Garvey taught his followers that one way to

break free of discrimination and injustice was for Black people to start their own businesses and hence become financially independent of the white establishment. But Garvey's most ambitious project was the Black Star Line, a shipping company intended to encourage trade among black entrepreneurs in America and the Caribbean. He and his followers bought three ships with this aim in mind, but was probably swindled in the process.

In 1920 the UNIA held its first international convention, and 25,000 people crowded into New York's Madison Square Garden. Uniformed members marched through the streets of New York, and the convention demanded equal rights for Black people throughout the world.

At the heart of Garvey's philosophy was the idea of 'African redemption' and the powerful slogan 'Africa for the Africans!' Garvey believed that Black people around the world should return to their ancestral African homelands, thereby escaping racism and beginning the reconstruction of a united African continent. It was soon known as the "Back to Africa Movement" and although the idea never really took shape, it exerted a powerful influence on many followers.

Such ideas were revolutionary in the 1920s, and Garvey gained many enemies. *The Negro World* was widely banned as subversive, and followers of Garvey were denied entry into several Caribbean territories. Some critics also accused him of being too interested in personal power and of encouraging a personality cult. Finally, in 1925, the US authorities arrested him on trumped-up charges of fraud concerning the Black Star Line and he was jailed for two years. When he was released, he returned to a hero's welcome in Jamaica, where he revived the UNIA and spoke to enthusiastic crowds: 'Therefore the American Negroes and the West Indian Negroes are one, and they are the relics of the great African race which was brought into the Western world and kept here for 300 years. I told them in Harlem that it was my duty to reunite the Negroes of the Western world with the Negroes of Africa, to make a great nation of Black men . . .' (The Ward Theatre, Kingston, 1927).

Forming the People's Political Party, Garvey won a seat on Kingston's Parish Council, but the authorities prevented him from taking it up. They were alarmed at his criticism of colonial rule and his demands for improved conditions and wages for Jamaica's workers. He tried to seek election to the island's legislative council, but at that time only a small minority of people were entitled to vote. Those who were enfranchised were mostly from the upper and middle classes, and Garvey's radical ideas were anathema to such people. He lost the election and his influence began to fade. The UNIA also lost momentum, especially when the Depression of the 1930s created mass unemployment throughout the Americas. In 1935 Garvey left Jamaica for the last time, sailing to England where he died in obscurity five years later.

Garvey's remains were brought back to Jamaica in 1964 and he was made a National Hero. He is now remembered as a man who tried to instill a sense of pride and purpose in Black people and as somebody who inspired following generations of civil rights activists and pan-Africanist politicians. Above all, he was responsible for creating an ideal and a dream shared by millions of people across the world.

DID YOU KNOW? Before leaving Jamaica for the last time, Garvey is said to have told his supporters to prepare for the coming of a black king in Africa. This prediction was to be important in the beliefs of the Rastafari movement, which saw in Ethiopia's Emperor Haile Selassie the promised African leader.

READ MORE: Rupert Charles Lewis, *Marcus Garvey: Anti-Colonial Champion* **(New Jersey: Africa World Press)**

George Padmore

1902-1959

Baptized 'the father of pan-Africanism', Padmore was one of the most influential of Black intellectuals and activists in the twentieth century. He acted as a catalyst, putting into contact leaders and thinkers from around the world. Although his political views and concept of strategy changed during his life, he remained totally committed to the vision of a free and independent Africa, liberated from European colonialism and internal divisions.

Like two other important pan-Africanists, C.L.R. James and Henry Sylvester Williams, Padmore was born in Trinidad. He was called Malcolm Nurse and was the son of a middle-class pharmaceutical chemist. In his youth he was friendly with James and the future Prime Minister of Trinidad and Tobago, Eric Williams. He, like many others of his generation, felt frustrated by the social and racial restrictions of colonial Trinidad and in 1924 he left for the US to study medicine at Fisk University. There, he came into contact with left-wing ideas and he joined the US Communist Party soon afterwards.

His rise through the Party's ranks was rapid, as he was an effective organizer and good speaker, and he became active in New York, joining the American Negro Labor Congress (ANLC) – a Communist-led organization that tried to attract Black workers. For four years he carried out political work in New York, writing for and editing the ANLC's newspaper *The Negro Champion* and taking part in militant rent strikes and boycotts in Harlem. These were dangerous days for Communists in the US as the Great Depression began to create unusual political tensions and increase the level of racism faced by many Black people.

African independence was one of his goals, but he also continued to take an interest in the Caribbean, supporting the idea of an inter-island federation to replace British colonial rule in Trinidad and elsewhere:

'The Federation of the British West Indies will undoubtedly make for the beginning of a nationalist movement . . . Those in this country can be depended upon to play an important role in helping their countrymen to foster such a forward movement . . . Their group life in America has tended to unite them, for it is the first time in the history of these peoples that they have been brought together. The Negro Champion stands ready to give its full support to a militant movement among the islanders for the federation and the freedom of the West Indies.'

In 1930, George Padmore (as he was by then known) left for Moscow to work full-time for the cause of world Communism. The Communist International had identified trade unions as a particular target for infiltration and propaganda at the time, and Padmore became

head of the Negro Department of the Communist Trade Union International. His task was to encourage the development of militant unions in Africa, the Caribbean and North America, so that Black workers around the world would be attracted to Marxist ideas. Padmore identified strongly with this strategy as it emphasized the fact that Black workers faced particular problems of colonial oppression and racism around the world. From his position in Moscow and working in places like Paris and Hamburg as well as London, he was able to establish an enormous number of political contacts and he organized an elaborate network of anti-colonial activists in Africa and the Caribbean. African students would arrive in London, meet Padmore and rapidly fall under his spell, embracing Marxism and the Communist interpretation of Black liberation. In 1931 Padmore wrote his influential *The Life and Struggles of Negro Toilers*, a book that exposed the exploitation of Black workers around the world. In 1932 he recruited the outstanding Black author, Richard Wright, to the Communist Party.

But Padmore and the Communist International were to part company in 1934 during a bitter argument over strategy. The Communists, alarmed at the rise of Fascism in Europe, had decided that it was safer to reduce their hostility towards Western capitalist countries such as Britain and the US and to form anti-Fascist alliances wherever possible. This meant that Padmore was instructed to stop his activities in the British colonies so that the Soviet Union could not be accused of encouraging unrest there. Padmore protested loudly that the Communists were betraying Black workers in the interests of short-term strategy, but to no avail. He was expelled from the Party in 1934 for 'an incorrect attitude to the national question'. In other words, he had wanted to continue the revolutionary struggle, while the Communists had wanted to form strategic alliances with the Western powers – with the result that revolution was no longer a priority. Padmore complained that the Communist International had planned to reduce its anti-colonial agitation 'in order not to offend the British Foreign Office which has been bringing pressure to bear on Soviet diplomacy because of the tremendous indignation which our work has aroused among the Negro masses in Africa, the West Indies and other colonies against British imperialism'.

After leaving the Soviet Union, Padmore eventually returned to London, without resources but determined to carry on the anti-colonial struggle. Making a meagre living from journalism, he continued to press for African independence, attending endless meetings and cultivating as many contacts as possible. It was during this period that I got to know him and became a regular visitor to his one-room flat. I remember above all his complete integrity and honesty. On one occasion, for instance, I was present when the British Colonial Secretary Arthur Creech-Jones, a former political acquaintance of Padmore, offered him a very lucrative job on the Colonial Office's ground nut scheme for East Africa. Padmore graciously refused the offer (even though he desperately needed the money), explaining that the scheme was ill-conceived and that the funds would be better spent on establishing an agricultural society among local farmers.

In the 1940s Padmore was instrumental in setting up the International African Service Bureau in London, a network that brought together activists from Africa and the

Caribbean and was hugely influential in promoting the idea of pan-African unity. His old friend C.L.R. James was active in the network as were numerous others who organized meetings, wrote letters and staged demonstrations against British colonialism. In 1945 Padmore was an important participant in the historic fifth pan-African Congress in Manchester. He had become a strong anti-Communist, later arguing in his book *Pan-Africanism or Communism* that Black people must be 'mentally free from the dictation of Europeans, regardless of their ideology'.

By now, Padmore had become a close associate of Kwame Nkrumah and he was an important influence during the decade between 1947 and 1957 when Nkrumah led the independence struggle that created the new state of Ghana. C.L.R. James wrote that 'it is impossible to understand the development of the revolution in the Gold Coast that brought Ghana, unless you realized from the start that the man behind it was Padmore'.

Once his friend and political colleague was installed as President of Ghana in 1957, Padmore left London to join him as a 'personal advisor'. There he continued to work alongside Nkrumah in encouraging independence movements in other African territories. Although there was some resentment among Ghanaians that a Trinidadian exerted such an influence on Nkrumah, Padmore did a great deal to promote Ghana as a leading nation in terms of African unity. He died only two years later, however, after a mysterious illness. According to James, the interment of his ashes attracted a huge crowd of Ghanaian mourners: 'Peasants from remote areas who, it could have been thought, had never heard his name, found their way to Accra to pay the last tribute to this West Indian who had spent his life in their service.'

As a man of ideas and deep convictions, Padmore also earned criticism, including the reproach that his hatred of Communism finally made him too tolerant of British and US imperialism. What is not in question, however, is his life-long commitment to Black liberation, whether among the workers of Harlem or the peasantry of Ghana.

DID YOU KNOW? Malcolm Nurse's choice of the pseudonym 'George Padmore' came about when he was consulting a friend about suitable names. She suggested Padmore after a Liberian Minister, and he responded 'By George, you've got it', thereby stumbling upon his new first name by accident.

READ MORE: George Padmore, *The Life and Struggles of Negro Toilers* (New York: Borgo Press)

C.L.R. James

1901-1989

Historian, novelist, critic, political activist and cricket enthusiast, Cyril Lionel Robert James was born in Tunapuna, near Port of Spain, Trinidad on 4 January 1901. The son of a schoolteacher and book-loving mother, he grew up surrounded by the works of Thackeray and Shakespeare. He did well at school, won a scholarship at the prestigious Queen's Royal College and became a teacher himself at the age of 19. He never lost his gift for teaching and was a sought-after lecturer and adviser for the whole of his life. Among his early pupils was the young Eric Williams, later to become independent Trinidad's first Prime Minister. James was also a keen cricketer and athlete, winning Trinidad's high jump championship.

Like many Caribbean intellectuals of his generation, James found colonial island life constricting and frustrating. His academic excellence was undoubted, but he still faced the barriers imposed by class and colour. In 1932 he left for Britain, to join his friend Learie Constantine, then a professional cricketer in Lancashire. It was the decisive step in his political development, as from the outside he was able to analyse the current situation in the Caribbean and increase his awareness of other issues. He found work as a cricket correspondent on the *Manchester Guardian*, but soon moved to London, where he was active in the growing pan-African movement.

James was completely in his element in the political ferment of 1930s London. His contacts included orthodox Communists such as George Padmore, Moscow's chief agent in charge of African and pan-African affairs and a wide variety of Trotskyists and other revolutionaries. With other intellectuals and activists, he debated the role of Marcus Garvey, the importance of the Harlem Renaissance and the revolutionary ideas of négritude, then being developed in Paris by writers such as Aimé Césaire and Léopold Senghor. It has been rightly said of his tremendous ability that 'his intellectual frontiers were never closed.' His influence among radical black thinkers, nationalists and Marxists, was enormous. His publisher, Frederick Warburg, recalled: 'If politics was his religion and Marx his god, if literature was his passion and Shakespeare his prince among writers, cricket was his beloved activity.'

In 1938, C.L.R. James published *The Black Jacobins*, probably his most important book and required reading for anyone interested in the history of Haiti and the Caribbean. In it he analysed how the slaves of French colonial Saint-Domingue endured an eleven-year civil war to drive out their oppressors and found free and independent Haiti. Central to the narrative is the figure of Toussaint L'Ouverture, the former slave and master tactician, who was

instrumental in ending colonial rule and slavery. This is a great piece of historical writing, but it also had a direct political message for the time in which it was written, for James was increasingly convinced that only revolution in Africa could end European colonialism there.

That same year, James moved to the US, where he became active in the Trotskyist Socialist Workers' Party. He was interned on Ellis Island in 1952 and was expelled the following year, returning to England. In 1958 he went to Trinidad and spent four years there in the period leading up to independence. During that time he was associated with Eric Williams, by now the leader of the People's National Movement (PNM). Attracted by the PNM's anti-imperialist stance, James became editor of the party newspaper, the *Nation*. Yet within two years he and Williams had split over ideological differences and James left Trinidad. From 1962 onwards, James was mostly based in London, where he died aged 88 in 1989. He was buried in the cemetery at Tunapuna, where his tombstone carries a quotation from his celebrated book on cricket, *Beyond a Boundary*: 'Times would pass, old empires would fall and new ones take their place, the relations of countries and the relations of classes had to change, before I discovered that it is not the quality of goods and utility which matter, but movements; not where you are or what you have, but where you have come from, where you are going and the rate at which you are getting there.'

James' stature as a leading twentieth-century Marxist thinker grew throughout his long and distinguished career. He was responsible for bringing together many different pan-Africanists, including Kwame Nkrumah, George Padmore and myself. He sent a cable to

Padmore in London from the US, telling him to meet Nkrumah when he arrived in Britain – a message that started the important relationship between the two of them. His intellectual curiosity encompassed many areas, including revolutionary politics, literature and, of course, cricket, and this helped him to place the Caribbean in proper perspective in world affairs. Africa – and the role of imperialism – remained a central theme in his thinking. He had no illusions about the challenges facing an independent post-colonial Africa, nor who was responsible for its many problems: 'Under the best of circumstances the future of Africa is a future of turmoil, stress and strain, revolution or counterrevolution, disputes between tribes and national units, complicated by the disputes between European powers and the Africans, and between the European powers themselves. It is a fantasy to believe that these imperialist powers are the ones who will guide Africa safely through these troubles. They are the ones responsible for them. They are the ones who are making it more difficult than ever for the Africans to find their own way.'

A particular source of inspiration for James was Kwame Nkrumah, who became the first leader of independent Ghana in 1957. James visited Nkrumah on several occasions and perceived his government as a possible blueprint for independence across Africa. Nkrumah was ousted by a military coup in 1966, however, and James analysed his rise and fall in the book *Nkrumah and the Ghana Revolution* (1977).

James was always a passionate advocate of political independence, not only in Africa, but also in the Caribbean. As far back as 1932 he was arguing that Britain and the other European powers should relinquish their rule over the region. He was an early supporter of the concept of federation, arguing that the small islands should join together in a political union. Self-government, he said, was the only possible means of bringing democracy and freedom to people, and for this reason, although a Marxist, he opposed the one-party state constructed in the Soviet Union. James may be said to have ignited the spark of West Indian nationalism and fanned its flames into a blazing torch which illuminated the entire region.

A prolific writer, James' many works include the novel *Minty Alley* (1936), the play *Toussaint L'Ouverture* (1936) and a collection of political and cricket writing, *Beyond a Boundary* (1963). *Beyond a Boundary* was described by the *Sunday Times* in London as 'the greatest sports book ever written'. Revealing James' deep love of the sport, it also uses cricket as a way of explaining Caribbean history and society. 'What do they know of cricket who only cricket know?' he asked, meaning that cricket in the region is much more than just a game. 'West Indians crowding to Tests bring with them the whole past history and future hopes of the islands', he concluded.

DID YOU KNOW? The leading actor in James's play *Toussaint L'Ouverture*, which started in London in 1936, was the great singer and pan-African Paul Robeson. The play was not a great success, however, and soon closed.

READ MORE: C.L.R. James, *The Black Jacobins* (London: Allison & Busby)

Kwame Nkrumah

1909-1972

Nkrumah is considered by many today to have been one of the brightest and most committed leaders ever produced by the African continent. From an early age he discovered that his task in life was to emancipate his people from the grip of colonialism. He understood and hated the very nature of imperialism, fighting it at every level. He believed without any doubt that until Africa was free from colonialism the struggle would have to continue.

Born on 21 September 1909 at Nkroful in what was then the British-ruled colony of the Gold Coast, Nkrumah was the son of a goldsmith. Although his family background was by no means prosperous, he was able to obtain a decent education and train as a teacher. So intelligent was the young Nkrumah that he managed to win a scholarship to the US, where he received a degree in 1939 from Lincoln University – the same university where Paul Robeson's father had studied. From there he moved to Britain, and it was there that I first met him.

At the time there was a group of us in London interested in Africa and pan-Africanism. I remember that I was at the flat of George Padmore when he received a cable from the US, sent by our associate C.L.R. James in New York, which read something like this: 'George, please arrange to meet a young African student from the Gold Coast who is arriving in England on . . . He is determined to rid Africa of the English.' George invited me to come along and I saw this handsome young African at Waterloo Station with his suitcase waiting for us. He was charming, intelligent and full of energy. There was an immediate chemical affinity between Padmore and Nkrumah, which lasted for the rest of their lives. Padmore was seven years older and acted as Nkrumah's mentor, while Nkrumah was like a dedicated student, eager for knowledge and unafraid to challenge the status quo.

From the outset, Nkrumah made it plain that his objective was nothing less than complete independence for the Gold Coast. 'No race, no people, no nation can exist freely or be respected at home or abroad without political freedom', he said, 'economic freedom must follow.'

At that time, goals such as this seemed very distant. Very few British colonies during the early 1940s had anything like universal suffrage and, apart from India, no colony was openly asking for its independence. It was to take many years of debate and political activity before Nkrumah's dream could become reality. In 1945, however, the British government announced that the end of the Second World War would witness an answer to growing anti-colonial opinion. Nkrumah was in two minds as to whether to return to Africa to become involved in the independence struggle there or whether to continue his studies in Britain. Before he left for Africa, he took part in the sixth pan-African Congress in Manchester, a gathering that brought together 94 delegates from Africa, the Caribbean and the US. Nkrumah later said that 'at Manchester, we knew that we were speaking for all Africa, expressing the deepest desires and determination of a mighty continent to be wholly free.'

After lengthy deliberations with Padmore, Nkrumah returned to the Gold Coast in 1947, joining the newly founded United Gold Coast Convention and rapidly rising through the ranks to become general-secretary. Frustrated by the slow pace of change and the caution of his colleagues, however, he broke away in 1949 to form the Convention People's Party (CPP) under the slogan 'Independence Now'. Supported by radical sectors in society and young people impatient for reform, Nkrumah led a 'positive action' campaign, which resulted in him being jailed by the British authorities in 1950. But the following year the CPP swept the board in elections and he was freed to form a government under a new, more liberal, constitution.

Nkrumah became the idol of his people, known as 'Osagyefo' (the Redeemer). Now in a position of power, he was able to accelerate the process that would lead to independence. He was also able to speak internationally for

the pan-African cause, representing his country (now known as Ghana) at the famous Bandung Conference in 1955 – a meeting that led to the founding of the Non-Aligned Movement. In 1957 independence was at last attained. The following year, Nkrumah spoke of his hopes for the future:

'For the first time, I think, in the history of this great continent, leaders of purely African states which can play an independent role in international affairs will meet to discuss the problems of our countries and take the first steps towards working out an African contribution towards international peace and goodwill. For too long in our history Africa has spoken through the voice of others. Now what I call an African personality in international affairs will have a chance of making its proper impact and will let the world know it through the voices of Africa's own sons.'

Nkrumah was able to put his radical brand of pan-Africanism into practice over the next decade, encouraging other African colonies to press for independence and supporting the Organization of African Unity that he helped found in 1963. He became an international figure, meeting world leaders such as Nasser, Nehru and Mao Tse Tung and representing Black Africa at many top-level meetings. He never forgot his own humble beginnings, nor the intellectual debt he owed to Marcus Garvey: 'But I think that of all the literature I have studied, the book that did more to me than any other to fuel my enthusiasm was "The Philosophy and Opinions of Marcus Garvey" (1923).' Nkrumah's tribute to Garvey was symbolized by the inclusion of Garvey's Black Star insignia in the new flag of the free Republic of Ghana.

At home, Nkrumah tried to introduce a

series of reforms, including breaking up large farms and distributing land to poorer peasants. He also believed that Ghana should develop its own industries and become more self-reliant. But these policies made him unpopular with the US and European powers as well as with tribalist opponents inside Ghana. The country faced an economic crisis when the prices fetched by commodities such as cocoa fell steeply on the world market. When Nkrumah went looking for loans abroad to help his government meet its commitments, they were provided only at high rates of interest. Even so, he created an education system that was the envy of other African states, built up the country's infrastructure and created the great Volta Dam, which made Ghana self-sufficient in electricity.

By 1966, however, his opponents were accusing him of becoming a dictator, as he had banned other parties and proclaimed himself president-for-life in 1964. The US government was only to willing to back anti-Nkrumah forces, and in 1966, while he was on a state visit to China, he was ousted by a military coup. Three years later, the military leaders allowed elections again, but stopped the CPP from taking part. Nkrumah lived the rest of his life in exile, first in Guinea and then later in Romania. He died on 27 April 1972 in a hospital in Bucharest.

Despite the controversy surrounding his methods in later years, Nkrumah is still remembered as the father of independent Ghana and one of the most articulate exponents of pan-Africanism. His dream of a 'United African States' was never fulfilled, but his vision inspired a generation of Africans to believe in the enormous potential of their continent.

DID YOU KNOW? Nkrumah developed the concept of 'neo-colonialism', meaning the relationship of inequality that exists after a country has granted political independence to a colony but continues to dominate its economy.

READ MORE: Kwame Arhin, *The Life and Work of Kwame Nkrumah* (New Jersey: Africa World Press)

44   *Julius Nyerere*

Julius Nyerere

1922-1999

Nyerere is a man of unusual sincerity and integrity – qualities which earned him the trust of his people throughout his long political career. He believed that equality lay at the heart of a just and harmonious society and worked hard to create the conditions for an original, African-based form of socialism. He also led a long struggle against the white racist societies of Rhodesia and South Africa, championing the cause of Black African unity.

Julius Kambarage Nyerere was born in March 1922 in Butiama in what was then British-ruled Tanganyika. The son of a minor chief of the Wazanaki people, he was educated in Catholic schools and then Makerere University in Uganda, training to be a teacher. After a period as a schoolmaster, he then went to Edinburgh University in Scotland, where he took a degree in Education in 1952.

When he returned home, he faced the choice of continuing as a teacher or developing his growing interest in politics into practical action. He chose the latter, spending the next two years travelling throughout Tanganyika in order to familiarize himself with its people and their problems. He discovered that the territory consisted of many different groups and peoples, divided by religion, customs and over 150 languages. At that time, Tanganyika was a British Trustee Territory, having formerly been a German colony, and was awaiting independence. Divided by their many tribal cultures, its people had little experience of political or social organizing.

Nyerere founded a political party, the Tanganyika African National Union (TANU) in 1954 and became its president. His aim was to unify his country's people and to offer them a sense of direction in the search for independence. He was immediately successful and began to win the respect and confidence of ordinary people by championing their causes. In the run-up to independence he made several visits to London and to the United Nations in New York to represent particular groups in Tanganyika who were disadvantaged or discriminated against in some way. One such cause was that of the Wameru tribe, who had been forcibly evicted from their traditional homeland and resettled elsewhere so that their land could be distributed to European settlers for coffee plantations. Accompanied by tribesmen, Nyerere argued persuasively for the rights of Africans in their own land.

TANU decided that it would be a primarily African party and admitted only Africans as members. This meant that the wealthiest inhabitants of the territory – Europeans and Asian-descended businessmen – were not allowed to join. As a result, TANU had little financial backing, but it appealed strongly to the poorest sectors in the country – peasant farmers and rural labourers. Throughout the 1950s Nyerere held meetings in every part of the country, introducing ideas of democracy and popular participation to people who had never heard of such ideas. He preached the doctrine of egalitarianism and the values of the traditional harmonious family, demonstrating that religious, class and tribal differences weakened the community and destroyed any prospect of a national movement.

Nyerere had solid links with other African leaders – Nkrumah in Ghana, Jomo Kenyatta in Kenya and Milton Obote in Uganda, and these links encouraged him to think in terms of pan-African unity. But his main priority was to create a united country out of Tanganyika's many tribes – a goal which became more achievable when TANU won elections in 1960 and Nyerere became the colony's chief minister. Independence followed smoothly the next year thanks to his close collaboration with the British authorities, and Nyerere continued as prime minister. In 1962, however, he resigned to concentrate on restructuring TANU for its post-independence role.

It was around then, before Nyerere became president, that I first met him. He came to visit me as a client in my lawyer's office at Moshi, a beautiful country hamlet in the foothills of Mount Kilimanjaro. My clerk told me that there was a gentleman waiting to see me but that he had allowed others to go ahead of him. We met and the chemistry worked at once. So intense and instructive was his conversation

that we continued it over dinner and long into the night. He is certainly one of the most remarkable men I have ever met. Since then, I have accompanied him on several unofficial visits and witnessed his capacity to put all sorts of people at ease, always meeting them with a smile on his face.

Shortly afterwards in late 1962, fresh elections brought Nyerere back to power as president of the Republic of Tanganyika. The following year an insurrection broke out on the offshore Arab-dominated island of Zanzibar, still under British rule. In 1964 the island joined Tanganyika in a new union and country, to be called Tanzania.

From 1964 until 1985, Nyerere was president of a united Tanzania and a tireless opponent of dictatorship and apartheid in Africa. He sent Tanzanian troops into Uganda to help overthrow the tyrannical Idi Amin. He also gave support to fighters from the African National Congress in South Africa as well as liberation forces in Zimbabwe, Mozambique and Angola. Instrumental in setting up the Organization of African Unity, Nyerere won an international reputation as a defender of African causes and a Third World leader.

In Tanzania itself Nyerere put into practice the idea of ujamaa or 'familyhood', a unique form of rural socialism. His vision of society was one in which, like the family, mutual respect and obligation bound members together, with a central authority or father figure acting as final arbiter. He made no excuses for running a one-party state, arguing that Tanzania's tribalism gave it no alternative but to have a single unifying sense of direction. Although Tanzania's economy suffered badly in the 1970s and ujamaa was thought by many to have failed, Nyerere has always defended the moral purpose and African nature of his social model.

'You have to understand the values of socialism which we were trying to build in Tanzania – the values of justice, a respect for human beings, a development which is people-centred, a development where you care about people. You can say you should leave the development of a country to something called "the market", which has no heart at all, since capitalism is completely ruthless. But who is going to help the poor? And remember that the majority of the people in our countries are poor. Who is going to stand up for them? Not "the market." So I don't regret that I tried to build a country based on those principles . . . When we have African problems, we ourselves have a duty to solve our own problems. I think we must accept that . . . We would prefer the outside world to keep out. If we want help, we can ask for help.'

In 1985 Nyerere – also known in Swahili as Mwalimu or Teacher – stood down from power, passing on the presidency to an elected successor. He has since remained active in African politics, working as an intermediary in the civil wars and genocide in Rwanda and Burundi. Although he may not have succeeded in bringing material prosperity to poor Tanzanians, he presided over the evolution of a strong sense of national identity which has not been undermined by ethnic unrest.

A naturally modest man of small stature, Nyerere practised what he preached and always lived an unostentatious life. He is one of the few world leaders whose manner, language and ideas instinctively attracted the masses to him. Using aphorisms and images from everyday African rural life, he was able to entertain as well as make important political points to his people. When, for instance, he wanted to explain how the poor usually pay for the differences between the rich, he memorably remarked: 'When the elephants fight, it is the grass that suffers. And even when they make love, it is the grass that suffers!'

DID YOU KNOW? Under Nyerere's leadership, Tanzania became the first country on the continent with a native African official language – Swahili. He also translated the works of Shakespeare into Swahili.

READ MORE: Colin Legum and Geoffrey Mmari, *Mwalimu: The Influence of Nyerere* (New Jersey: Africa World Press)

Jomo Kenyatta

1891?-1978

Jomo Kenyatta was a Kenyan patriot, who through his courage and political leadership helped his country to obtain its independence from Britain on 12 December 1963. His bravery and outspoken manner earned him the title of 'Mr Africa' in the 1950s and 1960s and he remained a larger than life character throughout his often controversial political career.

The date of Kenyatta's birth is not certain, but it was probably in October 1891 that Kamau wa Ngengi was born at Ichaweri in what was then British East Africa. He was a member of the Kikuyu tribe. Both his father and mother died when he was young and he lived with his grandfather, Kingu Magana, a medicine man and fortune-teller. In 1909 he joined the Church of Scotland Mission at Thogoto, where he received an elementary education before becoming an apprentice carpenter. In 1914 he was christened as John Peter Kamau but then changed his name to Johnstone Kamau.

After working as a farmhand, Kamau moved to Nairobi, where he became attracted to politics, joining the Kikuyu Central Association (KCA) in 1922. This organization campaigned on behalf of Black Africans against the racism and injustices that were perpetrated in the colony by the white minority and the authorities. The British government actively encouraged white settlers to establish vast plantations in the territory, and areas known as the 'White Highlands' were reserved for European farmers alone. As a result, the Kikuyu and other tribes lost thousands of acres of their ancestral lands and were forced to work for a pittance on the white-owned plantations. Gradually Kamau became more involved in the struggle for land rights and democrcacy and by 1928 he was travelling widely in the Kikuyu areas of the colony, setting up branches of the KCA.

In 1929 the KCA decided to send Kamau to Britain to publicize its cause and to put its grievances to the Colonial Office. It was there that I first met him and we became friends. He successfully informed the public about the injustices suffered by the Kikuyu people, but was ignored by a Parliamentary Commission set up to look into land rights in East Africa. He also studied at University College, London, where under Professor Bronislaw Malinowski he carried out the research for his influential book, *Facing Mount Kenya* (1938). It was at this stage that Kamau changed his name once more – to Jomo Kenyatta. The book was a great success, detailing daily life among the Kikuyu in a highly readable way. It also spoke of the way in which the Kikuyu had been dispossessed of their land and culture:

'When the missionaries arrived, the Africans had the land and the missionaries had the Bible. They taught us to pray with our eyes closed. When we opened them, they had the land and we had the Bible.'

Kenyatta, along with others like George Padmore, C.L.R. James, Kwame Nkrumah and Peter Abrahams from South Africa, was instrumental in organizing the 1945 sixth pan-African Congress in Manchester, which he later described as 'a landmark in the history of the African peoples' struggle for unity and freedom'. The following year he returned home to resume his political activities and in 1947 he was elected President of the Kenya African Union (KAU), the main political party committed to independence, African voting rights and the return of tribal lands.

Life at this time was difficult for Kenyatta and when I saw him in 1951, he seemed a lonely and disappointed man. Many people were growing frustrated at the slow pace of negotiations between pro-independence forces and the colonial authorities, and in 1952 the Mau Mau uprising gathered momentum. This was a rebellion carried out by a secret society of Kikuyu members, who attacked white settlers and those Blacks whom they saw as collaborators. The uprising heightened tension in the colony, and Kenyatta's KAU became split over whether to press ahead with peaceful tactics or whether to support the Mau Mau.

During this period, despite his own doubts, Kenyatta's popularity began to rise. People would walk great distances to hear him speak, and he was a flamboyant personality, with his leather jacket and a huge ring. Carrying a carved cane and wearing his trademark kinyata, he would speak eloquently in Swahili, Kikuyu or English. The authorities distrusted him, and I remember that he often had to ask permission to hold a meeting from some semi-literate white officer, who would interrogate him about the purpose of the meeting.

Finally, on 21 October 1952, Kenyatta was arrested on charges of being a ringleader in the Mau Mau conspiracy. This threat had been hanging over his head for some time, although he had always been careful to condemn political violence in his speeches. The following month his trial began in the remote village of Kapenguria near the Ethiopian border. I was part of his defence team of lawyers, a team including legal representatives from India, Nigeria and Britain. I was also able to attract interest and support from around the world by alerting political leaders to the significance of the trial. Nehru himself dispatched the eminent lawyer Chaman Lall to help with the defence. The trial was nothing short of a fiasco. The judge was a white planter, who clearly had his orders. In a travesty of justice, Kenyatta was sentenced to seven years hard labour and indefinite restriction after the prison sentence.

While Kenyatta served his sentence, the insurgency against British rule continued unabated. At the same time, calls for his release intensified. After seven years he was released from prison but was still kept under strict restrictions at the remote town of Lodwar. The campaign to free him gathered impetus. In 1960 over a million signatures were presented in a petition to the Governor, and in May that year Kenyatta was unanimously elected – in his absence – to the presidency of the renamed Kenya African National Union (KANU). In August 1961 the British authorities finally gave in to popular pressure and Kenyatta was freed to a hero's welcome across the country.

The movement towards independence now gathered pace, especially in the wake of Ghana's transition to independence in 1957. After a series of negotiations in London, Kenyatta led KANU to a sweeping victory in elections in May 1963. He preached reconciliation with the white minority, asking them to stay and cooperate in a free and independent Kenya. In December that year Kenyatta's dream was realized as the colony became the Republic of Kenya.

Known as Mzee (Swahili for 'respected elder'), Kenyatta ruled Kenya for fifteen years as prime minister and then president. He had many critics, who accused him of favouring his own Kikuyu supporters above other ethnic groups. He was also accused of pandering to foreign interests at the expense of poor Kenyans by allowing large companies to exploit the best farming land. But others, particularly the KANU faithful, revered him as the Father of the Nation. His doctrine of Harambee ('let us work together' in Swahili) emphasized tolerance and peace, and under his guidance Kenya was certainly a more stable country than many of its turbulent neighbours.

Kenyatta died on 22 August 1978 in Mombasa. A state funeral was attended by leaders from around the world. He was – and still is – remembered as a brave and charismatic leader, not without flaws, without whom the history of Kenya would have been very different indeed.

DID YOU KNOW? The adopted name of Jomo Kenyatta means 'burning spear' (Jomo), while Kenyatta refers to the beaded belt (kinyata) that he almost always wore.

READ MORE: Jomo Kenyatta, *Facing Mount Kenya* (New York: Vintage Books)

Haile Selassie I

1892-1975

The Emperor Haile Selassie I of Ethiopia occupies an important place in the history of Black people, not only for what he was – the head of a great African country – but also for the legacy he has left behind. He was baptized as Ras Tafari, and it is under that name that he is recognized as a God by Rastafarians around the world. He himself was a Christian and it is perhaps ironic that he never fully understood why Rastafari had evolved around his personality.

Ras Tafari was born on 23 July 1892 near Harar in Ethiopia, the son of Ras Makonnen, Governor of Harar province, and related to Emperor Menelik II. He was believed to be a direct descendant of the biblical King Solomon and the Queen of Sheba. Unusually for a member of the Ethiopian ruling caste, he was brought up with a wide and contemporary education, which included learning English and French as well as several Ethiopian languages. He also studied a great deal of holy writing. At the age of thirteen he was named Dejazmatch (literally, keeper of the door), a title equivalent to that of Count, for part of Harar province. A year later, his father died and he was looked after by his father's kinsman and friend, Menelik II. Ethiopian power

politics at the time were extremely complicated, with different noble families from different regions competing for control over the country as a whole. Ras Tafari became Governor of Harar and then Sidamo province before Menelik II died in 1913.

Upon Menelik II's death, the Empress Zauditu took power, with the 25-year-old Ras Tafari named as her regent. He remained in this position for the next thirteen years, during which as de facto ruler of Ethiopia he introduced wide-ranging reforms and modernized the country. Slavery was finally abolished in 1923 and Ethiopia was admitted into the League of Nations (the forerunner of the United Nations). The Regent was also responsible for building a modern education system and creating the beginnings of a national infrastructure of roads and communications. In response to his growing popularity, Zauditu crowned him Negus or King in 1928. But she was also jealous and suspicious of his influence and in 1930 Zauditu sent a large army to crush his local power base. The move failed, her troops were defeated by forces loyal to Ras Tafari and Zauditu died in mysterious circumstances days later.

The way was now clear for Ras Tafari to

take absolute power and in November 1930 he was crowned Emperor Haile Selassie I at a great ceremony in Addis Ababa. As Emperor he continued his reforming programmes, founding the Bank of Ethiopia in 1931 and encouraging a national media. His vision was to make Ethiopia a much stronger and more united country than had previously been the case, for he feared that outside powers might try to colonize the territory.

Such fears were justified, for in October 1935 Italy invaded Ethiopia. Italy had occupied neighbouring Eritrea from the 1890s, but under the Fascist dictator Benito Mussolini it had ambitions to expand its African empire. The war was a totally unequal one; the Italians had a modern army of planes, tanks and heavy weaponry, while the Ethiopians were mostly armed with spears and rifles. Using chemical weapons and heavy bombing, the Italians proved unstoppable and in May 1936 Haile Selassie was forced into exile first in Jerusalem and then Britain, where he appealed to the League of Nations to end the Italian occupation of his country. Prophetically, he warned that Fascism and military might would affect powerful nations as well as poor ones if the international community did nothing to resist leaders such as Mussolini and Hitler. 'Justice cannot be divided', he said, 'what is good for one is good for all and vice versa.'

The Second World War proved him right, but it also proved to be Italy's undoing, for when the Italians joined forces with Nazi Germany, Haile Selassie was able to collaborate directly with British forces in a plan to win back his country. From a base in Sudan he helped organize a force of British, South African and Ethiopian troops which re-entered Addis Ababa in May 1941.

Back in power after the war ended, Haile Selassie continued his modernization programme, reforming the legal system and bringing Ethiopia into the United Nations as a founder member. After centuries of relative isolation, the country established diplomatic links around the world and the Emperor travelled widely. He made many important and influential speeches during the 1950s and 1960s, including a famous attack on racism delivered to the UN in October 1963: '. . . Until the philosophy which holds one race superior and another inferior is finally and permanently discredited and abandoned. That until there are no longer first-class and second-class citizens of any nation. Until the colour of a man's skin is of no more significance than the colour of his eyes. That until the basic human rights are equally guaranteed to all, without regard to race. Until that day, the dream of lasting peace and world citizenship and the rule of international morality will remain but a fleeting illusion to be pursued but never attained . . .'

The Emperor survived a military coup attempt in 1960 while he was travelling in Brazil, but this event suggested that there was opposition to his rule. This opposition grew in the late 1960s and early 1970s as an attempt to introduce a sweeping land reform failed because of the grip on parliament by rich landowners. The economy began to fail, with high inflation, and a series of terrible droughts and famines affected the countryside. Gradually, opposition mounted and critics of Haile Selassie's absolute rule accused him and his followers of corruption and greed while the poor were starving.

I happened to be in Addis Ababa in September 1974, when a rebellion against the

Emperor broke out. Elements of the armed forces had mutinied the previous January and although they claimed allegiance to the Emperor, they began arresting politicians and people associated with Haile Selassie. Along with other members of the diplomatic corps, I had to hurry to escape, as the Emperor had said that he could not guarantee our safety as the military fought to take power once and for all. He was arrested on 12 September along with members of his family and died in August 1975 as a result of repeated torture. When the military dictatorship that followed was finally overthrown, his secret grave was found and it was discovered that the torturers had broken almost every bone in the Emperor's body.

It was a terrible end for a man venerated as a God by the religious movement known as Rastafari. This had grown up from the 1930s onwards, based on the belief that Ethiopia was a heaven on earth, that Haile Selassie was a living God and that all Black people would one day escape from exile in 'Babylon' and return to Africa. Influenced by the 'Back to Africa' doctrine of Marcus Garvey, Rastafarians believed that the white colonial powers had conspired to conceal the real truth contained in the Bible for the purpose of enslaving Africans.

Leaving aside his religious significance as 'Jah' in the Rasta system of beliefs, Haile Selassie was an important spokesman for African unity and a fierce opponent of racism and apartheid in South Africa. He was also responsible for beginning the modernization of what was essentially a feudal country in the 1920s and laying the basis for a modern nation state in Ethiopia.

DID YOU KNOW? Haile Selassie visited Jamaica in April 1966, where he was greeted by thousands of Rastafarians, acclaiming him as the returned Messiah. He granted some land at Shesemane near Addis Ababa to Jamaican settlers who wanted to live in what they saw as the promised land.

READ MORE: Nathaniel Murrell (ed), _Chanting Down Babylon: The Rastafari Reader_ (Kingston: Ian Randle Publishers)

Paul Robeson
1898-1976

A man of extraordinary conviction and courage, Paul Robeson was a multitalented individual: sportsman, actor, singer and political activist. Through his long, distinguished and often controversial career, he never lost his belief in racial and social equality and his hostility to all forms of oppression. Charming and charismatic, he was larger than life and stood tall for the advancement of Black people.

Born on 9 April 1898 in Princeton, New Jersey, Robeson was the son of an ex-slave who had escaped from Virginia in 1860 via the Underground Railway. William Drew Robeson was a source of inspiration to his son, since by hard work and determination he had then taken a degree at Lincoln University and become a minister of religion. Paul's earliest exposure to 'the music of his people' took place in the small Presbyterian churches of New Jersey where his father preached. Life was not easy, however, and Paul's father had to take many menial jobs in order to feed his family. Tragedy struck when Paul was six, his mother dying from burns after a piece of charcoal from their winter stove set fire to her dress. But Paul recalled that he never saw his father express any bitterness or self-pity. Instead, he encouraged his son to stand up for his principles and to achieve his aims through hard work and perseverance.

Graduating from high school, Robeson won a scholarship to Rutgers University, where he studied law and won a reputation as an outstanding athlete, playing baseball, basketball and football. From there he moved to Harlem, where he enrolled in the law department of Columbia University. His father had died in 1918, and Robeson supported himself by working as a professional football player before gaining an honours degree in 1923. During that period he met and married Eslanda Cardozo Goode, who was instrumental in persuading him to take his first amateur acting role at the YWCA in Harlem in 1921.

This performance was to prove a turning-point in Robeson's life, and the following year he appeared on the professional stage and also performed as a singer in a vocal quartet. By 1924 he had given up the legal profession altogether, and in 1925 he played one of his most celebrated roles in *The Emperor Jones*. A series of highly acclaimed theatrical performances followed: *Show Boat* (1928), *Othello* (1930) and *Stevedore* (1935). He also appeared in eleven films between 1924 and 1942. Such was the quality of his acting in the role of *Othello* that the critic for *Variety* magazine concluded:

'Robeson's performance is of such a stature that no white man should ever dare to presume to play it again.'

Robeson also launched a successful professional singing career in 1925, and in 1927 he left the US for a two-year concert tour of Europe. In 1928 he settled in London, and from then on began commuting between the US and Europe. His singing introduced Black spirituals to an international audience, making songs like *Ol' Man River* known worldwide. Not only did Robeson reveal to the world the musical richness of Black American culture, but he also used these songs of suffering and hardship to draw people's attention to the fact that discrimination and racial violence were still part of everyday life in parts of the US.

It was following a visit to the Soviet Union in 1934 that politics began to feature prominently in Robeson's life and work. He had already had plenty of experience of racism and segregation in the US and had found Britain's old-fashioned class system to be repressive. In the 1920s he had become interested in the history and culture of Africa and was already making links between the position of Blacks in the US and the need for independence on the African continent. But the 1930s was a period in which politics took on a new urgency, with the rise of fascism in Germany, and Robeson looked to the Soviet Union and communism as the only real alternative. He was also conscious that his role as an artist and celebrity brought him special responsibilities: 'The artist must fight for freedom or for slavery . . . I have made my choice', he announced in 1937.

After involvement on the Republican side during the Spanish Civil war, Robeson returned to the US to contribute to the war effort. He entertained troops and recorded patriotic songs, winning government recognition and a series of awards.

But the anti-Communist atmosphere of the post-war years changed official attitudes towards Robeson and his outspoken support for the Soviet Union. He appeared in front of the Un-American Activities Committee in 1946 and then faced government harassment, censorship and even violence. He received death threats from the Ku Klux Klan, was banned from appearing on television and had his US passport cancelled. Even so, he courageously continued to speak out on Black and civil rights issues, supporting trade unions and pro-African groups with concerts and donations.

By the 1940s, Robeson was an international star and an influential advocate of pan-Africanism. He was an associate of W.E.B. Dubois and members of the Harlem Renaissance. He knew C.L.R. James and performed in a play he had written, and he was friendly with such African leaders as Kwame Nkrumah and Julius Nyerere. When he travelled to the Caribbean in 1949, he was received as a hero, saying 'If I never hear another kind word again, what I received from my people here in the West Indies will be enough for me.'

The witch hunt against Robeson and other Communist sympathizers continued throughout the 1950s, but he refused to moderate his statements or abandon his convictions. Instead, he emphasized his commitment not just to the Black cause, but to the cause of working people and the oppressed around the world.

'Even as I grew to feel more Negro in spirit, or African as I put it then, I also came to feel a sense of oneness with the white working people whom I came to know and love. This belief in the oneness of humankind has existed within

me side by side with my deep attachment to the cause of my own race. Some people have seen a contradiction in this duality. I do not think, however, that my sentiments are contradictory; I learned that there truly is a kinship among us all, a basis for mutual respect and brotherly love.'

Finally, after campaigns from Black American groups and supporters around the world, Robeson's passport was restored in 1958 and he was allowed to travel again. On his sixtieth birthday that year, some 27 countries honoured him with concerts and other festivities. The Prime Minister of India, Jawaharlal Nehru, paid tribute 'not only because Paul Robeson is one of the greatest artists of our generation, but also because he has represented and suffered for a cause which should be dear to all of us – the cause of human dignity.'

In 1961, Robeson became seriously ill and was treated in a Moscow hospital. The following year he decided to retire from public life. He lived his remaining years quietly in Philadelphia before dying on 28 December 1976. His wife had died in 1965, and he then lived with his sister, Marion Forsythe. A huge crowd attended his funeral in Harlem, probably remembering his words: 'Don't mourn for me, but live for freedom's cause.'

DID YOU KNOW? Paul Robeson was a natural linguist, who could speak and write in twenty languages, including Chinese, Russian, Arabic and several African languages.

READ MORE: Martin Duberman, *Paul Robeson: A Biography* (New York: New Press)

Rosa Parks

Rosa Parks

1913-

It does not happen often that an individual's action changes the course of history, but in Rosa Parks's case, this is precisely what happened. Her courageous act in December 1955 unleashed a series of events that had a profound impact in the southern states of the US and America as a whole. Today, she is honoured as somebody who took a principled stand against segregation and injustice.

Rosa Parks was born in 1913 and was brought to Montgomery, Alabama, two years later by her mother, Leona (Edwards) McCauley, when she separated from her husband. Rosa and her brother only rarely saw their father, James McCauley, who moved to the North, but they grew up among a tight-knit family of uncles, aunts, cousins and grandparents. Rosa's mother was a school-teacher, and she received her education at home until, at the age of eleven, she went to Montgomery Industrial School for Girls. That school, like the Booker T. Washington High School which she also attended, was for Black children only.

Almost all areas of life were segregated in Alabama in the first half of the twentieth century. Schools, other public buildings, hotels, restaurants and buses all had designated areas for Blacks and whites. Blacks were always treated as second-class citizens and their schools were run down and under-funded. Rosa Parks later recalled that some Black schools did not even have proper desks. While white children had buses to take them to school, many Black children like Rosa had to walk miles, often in the rain. Many of her friends did not go to school at all and grew up unable to read and write. But Rosa's grandfather taught her always to keep learning as the only way to be respected and treated as an equal. Even worse than the segregation was the violence and intimidation handed out by the Ku Klux Klan who had many followers in Alabama among white racists. They would terrify Black families by burning down their houses and often murdering individuals for no reason at all.

Rosa grew up in this atmosphere of racial hatred and became accustomed to obeying the segregation laws, even though she found them humiliating. When she was twenty, she married Raymond Parks, who worked as a barber, and they rented a house together. Rosa made money as a seamstress, but she was becoming increasingly interested in politics and civil rights and she joined the National

Association for the Advancement of Colored People (NAACP), working as secretary of the Montgomery branch.

By 1955 Rosa Parks was a respected activist in the NAACP who had grown used to opposing segregation in small but significant ways. She tried to register to vote on several occasions, despite the obstacles that were put in the way of Black people, and she was active in the Montgomery Voters League – a body that encouraged Blacks to register. She would avoid riding in Black-only elevators wherever possible by using the stairs and often had disagreements with the drivers of segregated buses. She later recalled: 'I didn't want to pay my fare and then go around the back door, because many times, even if you did that, you might not get on the bus at all, They'd probably shut the door, drive off and leave you standing there.'

Buses were a particular source of resentment for Black people, as the law stated that the front four rows of seats were reserved for white passengers and that Blacks had to sit at the back, even when their section was crowded and the white-only seats were empty. Furthermore, if the white seats were full, Blacks were obliged to give up their seats to any white passenger. Not surprisingly, many Blacks – who paid the same fare as whites – preferred to avoid using buses.

On 1 December 1955, Rosa Parks decided to take the bus home after a long day in the department store where she worked as a seamstress. She was sitting in the middle section with several other Black passengers when a white man boarded the bus and, noticing that the front four rows were occupied, demanded that all those sitting in her row go to the back of the vehicle. The others obeyed, but Rosa stayed put. 'My feet are tired', she said. And by that she meant more than a simple statement of fact, for what she was really telling the white man, the driver and the authorities was that she was tired of segregation and racial bigotry.

'Our mistreatment was just not right, and I was tired of it. I kept thinking about my mother and my grandparents, and how strong they were. I knew there was a possibility of being mistreated, but an opportunity was being given to me to do what I had asked of others.'

The white driver threatened to call the police, but Rosa calmly replied 'Go ahead and call them'. She was arrested, taken to the police station and jailed. With her one allowed telephone call, she contacted an NAACP lawyer who arranged her release on bail.

As word of Rosa's arrest spread, community leaders such as Martin Luther King, Jr. went into action to organize a campaign against segregation. The Montgomery Improvement Association was formed to lead a boycott of the bus company, and leaflets were distributed in Black neighbourhoods asking people not to use the buses until the segregation rules were scrapped.

The boycott lasted 382 days, causing the bus company to lose huge amounts of revenue. In the meantime, Rosa was fined for breaking a city ordinance, but her lawyers advised her not to pay so that they could challenge the segregation laws in court. A year after the boycott began, the US Supreme Court ruled that Alabama's segregation laws were indeed illegal. It was an enormous victory for the civil rights movement and a major step in the career of Martin Luther King, who went on to be the foremost spokesman for racial equality in the US until his assassination in 1968.

Rosa Parks has been called 'the mother of

the civil rights movement' and has been widely honoured in the decades following her courageous action. But life has been far from easy, as her fame also brought her harassment and threats from white racists. She was unable to keep her job and she and her husband moved to Detroit, where in 1965 she was offered a job on the staff of Congressman John Conyers. She retired in 1988 but continued to work on behalf of the Black community, establishing the Rosa and Raymond Parks Institute for Self-Development, a training centre for Detroit teenagers.

In August 1994, Americans were shocked to hear that the 81-year-old Rosa Parks had been attacked by a young unemployed burglar who robbed her of $53. She said of this incident: 'I pray for this young man and the conditions in our country that have made him this way.'

When I last saw her recently, she seemed a little tired and frail. She told me that her life consisted mainly of speaking at meetings and receiving honours. But these honours are well-deserved since her moment of courage started a movement that eventually changed the face of the US. Today many people can live without daily fear or hatred because of four little words – 'my feet are tired'.

DID YOU KNOW? In June 1999 Rosa Parks was awarded the Congressional Gold Medal, the highest civilian award given by the US Congress. Other recipients include Nelson Mandela and Mother Theresa.

READ MORE: Faith Ringgold, *If a Bus Could Talk: The Story of Rosa Parks* (New York: Simon & Schuster)

Martin Luther King, Jr.

1929-1968

Probably the most famous and inspiring Black American leader of the twentieth century, Martin Luther King, Jr. was directly responsible for important changes in US politics and society, bringing to an end the segregation laws that existed in some southern states and pressing for equality of voting rights between Blacks and whites. In a period of US history rife with violence, King stood out as an advocate of peaceful resistance and non-violent mass demonstrations. A man of enormous courage and dedication, he paid for his dream of racial and social equality with his life.

Born on 15 January 1929 in Atlanta, Georgia, Martin Luther King, Jr. was initially named Michael after his father, a minister at the Ebenezer Baptist Church. Growing up with his mother, Alberta, his father and his brother and sister, King was taught from an early age about Christian morality, justice and the importance of respecting other people. His father was an important figure in Atlanta's Black community and he preached regularly that Black Americans should have the same rights as whites and that they could begin to win such rights by obtaining the vote. But the young King could not help but notice that equality was only a dream and that segregation took many forms. As a child he was particularly friendly with a white boy, but when they reached school age, it became apparent that they had to go to different schools. After his first day at school, King was never allowed to play with his friend again.

When M.L. (as he was known by friends and family) left school, he decided to follow in his father's footsteps and become a Baptist minister. It was during his studies at the Crozer Theological Seminary in Pennsylvania that he came across the work of Mahatma Gandhi, the Indian leader who had organized the struggle against British rule in his country by 'passive resistance' and 'peaceful revolution'. This vision of a non-violent but politically effective mass campaign was to have a profound influence on King's thinking. He went on to take his Ph.D in theology in 1954, the year after he married Coretta Scott. That year he also started preaching at the Dexter Avenue Baptist Church in Montgomery, Alabama.

Almost immediately, Dr King's life was to become dominated by civil rights issues and political action. Barely a year after he began as a minister, Rosa Parks was arrested in Montgomery for failing to give her seat to a white man on a segregated bus. King knew her already and was eager to help mount a campaign to scrap the segregation laws. It was also an opportunity to put into practice the theory that mass peaceful action could bring about change. Without any doubt, the boycott organized by King was a complete success, and the bus laws were ruled illegal by the US Supreme Court after a year-long campaign. It was King's first civil rights victory, but already he was attracting enemies as well as admirers. In January 1956 his home was firebombed by unknown attackers.

Encouraged by the experience in Montgomery, Black church leaders formed the Southern Christian Leadership Conference in January 1957, with the aim of forcing changes to the voting system. This system openly discriminated against uneducated and poor Blacks by insisting on certain qualifying conditions such as literacy tests. The SCLC elected King as its President and he began to organize a series of peaceful mass demonstrations, including a march of 37,000 people to the Lincoln Memorial in Washington, DC, the following May. In that year King travelled an estimated 780,000 miles and made no fewer than 208 speeches as the main spokesman for Black civil rights.

In response to this growing movement, the US Congress created the Civil Rights Commission in September 1957, with the task of looking at voting laws and alleged discrimination. Led by King, the SCLC carried on its campaign, protesting against electoral irregu-larities, segregation and poor housing and education for Black people. In the course of this campaigning he developed his reputation as an exceptional speaker, who combined passion and common sense in a way that appealed to ordinary people. Crowds flocked to hear him wherever he spoke and soon he was exhausted by continual invitations to address meetings. In 1958 he decided to spend less time on the road and wrote a book, *Stride Toward Freedom*, which was a huge success. But in a sign of what was still to come, King was attacked in a Harlem bookshop by a Black woman when signing copies and badly wounded.

1959 marked an important event in King's life when he and his wife travelled to India, the homeland of Mahatma Gandhi, who had been assassinated in 1948. There he studied Gandhi's doctrine of satyagraha or non-violent persuasion. Upon his return to the US, he took up the position of minister at his father's church in Atlanta, sharing ministerial duties with Martin Luther King, Sr. From here he re-launched his civil rights activities, meeting with President John F. Kennedy to urge his support for an ending to discrimination. In 1963 the struggle against segregation entered a more militant phase as he led protests in Birmingham, Alabama, against segregated department stores and discriminatory employment practices. Demonstrators were attacked by police with tear gas and dogs, winning wide public support for King and his freedom fighters.

In August 1963, King's campaigning reached a climax as he spoke to a crowd of 200,000 at the Lincoln Memorial on the 100th anniversary of the Emancipation Proclamation that ended slavery in the US. It was here that he made his most famous speech, "I Have a Dream":

"I have a dream that my four children will one day live in a nation where they will not be judged by the color of their skin but by the content of their character. I have a dream. I have a dream that one day the state of Alabama, whose governor's lips are presently dripping with the words of interposition and nullification, will be transformed into a situation where little black boys and little black girls will be able to join hands with little white boys and white girls and walk together as sisters and brothers."

The impetus carried on into the following year when King was awarded the Nobel Peace Prize as somebody who 'had contributed the most to the furtherance of peace among men.' Typically, he donated his prize money to civil rights organizations. But King's actions were not always met with peace by his opponents. Demonstrations in Montgomery in 1965 ended in extreme violence from state troopers, who killed two ministers and injured seventy more. That same year, however, King witnessed perhaps his greatest achievement – the passing of the Voting Rights Act in Congress, a bill which abolished racial discrimination in voter registration.

By 1968 King was an enormously respected and charismatic leader. He also had many enemies, not just white racists but those who disapproved of his outspoken opposition to the Vietnam War. King believed that poverty and injustice were not just experienced by Black Americans, but by other oppressed peoples in the US and around the world. In April of that year he went to Memphis, Tennessee, to lend his support to striking workers. On 3 April he made a famous and strangely prophetic speech on the theme of the 'promised land': 'I may not get there with you. But I want you to know tonight that we, as a people, will get to the promised land. And I'm not fearing any man.' The next day, Dr Martin Luther King, Jr. was shot dead in the street by James Earl Ray.

Since his tragic death, King has come to symbolize all the positive aspects of the civil rights movement, with its emphasis on persuasion, moral justice and non-violence. An inspiration to succeeding generations of African Americans, he is also remembered as one of the finest and most moving orators of the modern age, for whom words were more effective weapons than physical force.

DID YOU KNOW? Since 1986, Martin Luther King's birthday in January has been celebrated as a national holiday across the US.

READ MORE: Clayborne Cardon (ed), *The Autobiography of Martin Luther King, Jr.* (New York: Warner Books)

Muhammad Ali

1942-

Three-time heavyweight boxing champion of the world, Muhammad Ali was one of the greatest boxers ever to appear in the ring. He was noted for his speed and accuracy as well as his mental agility and his ability to gain the psychological upper hand over his opponents. He became an international celebrity and brought a new popularity to the sport. But he was also a champion of Afro-American rights and an important spokesman for Blacks in the US and elsewhere in the world.

Born in Louisville, Kentucky on 17 January 1942, Cassius Marcellus Clay Jr. was the son of poor parents. He started boxing at the age of twelve, reputedly after his bicycle was stolen by neighbourhood bullies. From the outset, it was clear that the boy was both intelligent and athletic, and he rapidly established a reputation in amateur boxing, winning 103 out of 108 fights. He won the national Golden Gloves title twice, the AAU title twice, and then went on to win the 1960 Rome Olympic gold medal in the light heavyweight division.

After going as far as he could as an amateur, he then decided to turn professional and soon won a reputation as a flamboyant but ruthless boxer who could compete with the best. In 1964, after only twenty professional fights, he took on the fearsome Sonny Liston, the ex-convict who had defeated Floyd Patterson two years earlier to become heavyweight champion of the world. Few experts thought that the fast-talking young Cassius Clay, who dubbed himself 'the greatest', would stand a chance against Liston, with his knock-out punching, who had easily fended off other challenges to his crown. But the younger man won, outpacing Liston and tiring him out with his dazzling footwork. To the amazement of many, he forced Liston to retire from the fight after the sixth round.

The year 1964 was important in another way, for it was then that Cassius Clay announced to the world that he had become a Muslim, was now a member of the Nation of Islam, and would henceforth be known as Muhammad Ali. 'I had to prove you could be a new kind of black man', he told a biographer, 'I had to show that to the world.' At that time, Ali became friendly with Malcolm X and became involved in Black civil rights issues. These developments increased his popularity among more radical Black Americans, but soon brought him into conflict with mainstream America and the US government. He had earlier been hailed as a national hero, but the

decision to express his Black identity in what was seen as a politically controversial fashion led to personal and professional difficulties.

In the mid-1960s the US was deeply involved in the Vietnam War, and hundreds of thousands of Americans – many of them Black – were called up each year to fight. When Ali received his call-up papers in 1967, he refused to join the US military, claiming that he was a Black Muslim minister of religion and hence a conscientious objector. 'Man', he said, 'I ain't got no quarrel with them Vietcong.' To the many people around the world who saw the Vietnam War as an unjust conflict between a small nation and an interfering superpower, Ali's position was brave and correct. But to most Americans, this was seen as an act of treason. A court ruled that he was guilty of illegally evading the draft and he was sent to prison and fined $10,000. He was also ignominiously stripped of his title, which was declared vacant. The authorities finally banned him from fighting altogether, a move which cost Ali an estimated $10 million in lost income.

After three years in the wilderness (years that might have been his best in terms of his boxing career), Ali finally succeeded in having his conviction overturned by the US Supreme Court, which ruled against the lower court's judgment. By now, the Vietnam War was becoming increasingly unpopular among most Americans, and Ali was no longer viewed as suspect by opposing it. He returned to the ring in 1970 and won his first two fights, but when he tried to challenge the heavyweight champion, Joe Frazier, in March 1971, he lost. It was called 'the fight of the century', and Frazier finally won on points, having knocked Ali down in the 15th round.

It took another three years before Ali could stage another championship bid, defeating Frazier in January 1974 and then beating the then champion, George Foreman, in Kinshasa, Zaire, the following October. The so-called 'rumble in the jungle' was one of the most watched fights on TV in history. Tiring Foreman with his 'rope-a-dope' technique, Ali stopped the champion in the eighth round. Four years later in February 1978, Ali lost his title to another ex-Olympic medallist Leon Spinks in Las Vegas, who was fighting only his eighth professional fight. But Ali bounced back the following September to reclaim the championship for the third – and record – time in New Orleans.

Muhammad Ali retired in 1979, but decided the following year, perhaps unwisely, to challenge Larry Holmes, a former sparring partner, for the WBC heavyweight title. He was past his best and lost. His last fight was the following year, when he took on – and lost to – Trevor Berbick, a future champion.

Boxing took its toll on Ali, and his later years have been overshadowed by Parkinson's Disease. He now lives on his farm in Michigan. But he remains one of the ultimate sporting icons of the last century, combining superb boxing skills with a colourful personality uncommon for a professional boxer. Boxing was one area in American life in which Blacks were allowed and even expected to excel, but Ali was no ordinary Black boxer. He was charismatic, even arrogant, predicting the round in which he would beat an opponent and composing provocative poetry to try to upset his adversaries. Each fight was always preceded by Ali's press conferences, which turned into exhibitions of his quick wit and instinctive ability to manipulate the media. A poem was always composed for the occasion:

"This is the legend of Muhammad Ali,
The most popular fighter that ever will be;
He talks a great deal and brags indeed
Of a powerful punch and blinding speed;
The fistic world is dull and weary;
With a champ like Foreman, things got to
  be dreary!"

Ali's poem before the 1974 Foreman tie

Yet Ali was not just a great showman; his timing was perfect, and he often boxed one-handed, ducking to avoid punches and dancing around the ring. In his own immortal phrase, he could 'float like a butterfly, sting like a bee.'

Since his retirement, Ali has remained committed to human rights and Black issues, intervening during the Gulf War on humanitarian grounds and campaigning against Third World debt. He has used much of his fortune to help disadvantaged people of all backgrounds. In 1996, despite ill health, Ali was invited to perform the opening torch light ceremony at the Olympic Games.

DID YOU KNOW? Ali's 1974 heavyweight fight with Foreman in Kinshasa was the first world championship contest to be staged in Africa.

READ MORE: David Remnick, *King of the World: Muhammad Ali and the Rise of an American Hero* (New York: Random House)

Patrice Lumumba

1925-1961

Patrice Lumumba was one of Africa's most promising young leaders. A patriot and fierce opponent of imperialism in his native Congo, he was briefly the moving force behind his country's independence. But his ideas of national self-determination and social equality earned him many powerful enemies and he paid for his bravery with his life.

Lumumba was born in Katako Kombe, in the Congolese province of Kasai. Educated at a mission school, he was an intelligent child who seemed destined to leave his humble background behind him. After leaving school, he had several jobs, working as a nurse's assistant, a postal clerk and a volunteer librarian. All these experiences brought him into direct contact with poor people in the countryside and he gradually learned a great deal about their problems and hopes.

At that time, Congo was a Belgian colony, its vast mineral wealth being jealously guarded by the European colonists. Copper was the main export commodity and was largely to be found in the southern province of Katanga. The copper wealth may have made a handful of mining companies very wealthy, but it did almost nothing for the great majority of Congolese, who lived in extreme poverty in small villages or in the capital Kinshasa. The Belgians had also managed to secure their position of power in the territory by encouraging inter-tribal divisions as a way of ensuring that they could 'divide and rule'. Huge differences existed between the white colonists and their small elite of local associates and millions of Congolese, who were kept marginalized from economic and political power.

Against this background, the young Lumumba became interested in trade unionism as a way of mobilizing local people against the colonial system. He became secretary, then president, of the Association for African Government Employees and founded the Post Office Employees Club. At the same time, he was becoming increasingly convinced that living standards in his country could only be raised if the wealth from copper and other exports stopped flooding overseas. He had by now won a reputation as a confident organizer and an inspiring orator, talking to large crowds about his vision for the future. This future involved what were essentially modest demands, but they seemed almost revolutionary in colonial Congo. He called for improved salaries for public workers, better conditions for farmers, government investment in housing and education and a new relationship – built on equality and respect – between Belgium and the Congo. Most importantly, he rejected the old tribal and regional divisions and spoke of a united country.

In October 1958 Lumumba formed his own political party, the National Congolese Movement (MNC) and became its president. More liberal policies from Belgium had recently permitted the formation of political parties, and there were many tribal-based movements, but Lumumba's was the only party to be national in outlook and to favour independence from Belgium. The following December, Lumumba addressed the pan-African Conference in Accra, Ghana, where his attitude against Belgium hardened still further. This exposure to radical ideas from around the continent seemed to have a profound influence on him, and subsequently the MNC became explicitly pro-independence, whereas before Lumumba had actively sought the cooperation of Belgium in the creation of a more just society.

Independence came more quickly than Lumumba or anyone else had imagined. A peaceful political rally in 1959 was brutally crushed by the police, causing controversy around the world. Belgium was embarrassed by the incident and decided that granting political independence would not necessarily mean giving up its extensive economic interests. In 1960, the Belgians agreed to Congolese independence after elections had brought the MNC to power as the largest party in a coalition government. Lumumba was named prime minister.

King Baudouin of Belgium arrived in June that year to grant the Congo its freedom. In a patronizing speech, he said 'It is now up to you, gentlemen, to show that you are worthy of our confidence.' An angry Lumumba retorted that 'from this day the people of the Congo will no longer be satisfied to be treated as monkeys in their own land'. He went on to make a powerful speech: 'our lot was eighty years of colonial rule . . . We have known tiring labour exacted in exchange for a salary which did not allow us to suffer our hunger . . . We have known sarcasm, insults, blows which we had to endure morning, noon and night because we were "Negroes" . . . We have known that there were magnificent houses for the whites in the cities and tumble-down straw huts for the Negroes.'

Although he later apologized to the King for this outburst, the battle lines were clearly drawn.

By now, Lumumba was regarded with suspicion and hostility not just by Belgium, but also by the US, which was frightened that Communism might take root in Africa and threaten its interests there. Lumumba was not a Communist, but he spoke of the need for the Congo to control its own economy and to sever economic links with the old colonial power. When Europe and the US refused to grant the Congo aid, Lumumba looked to the Soviet Union – a move that frightened the US even more.

Soon after independence, the new nation of the Congo began to fall apart. First there was a mutiny by the local militia against the government. Then the copper-rich region of Katanga proclaimed in July 1960 that it was seceding from the Congo to become a separate country. There is no doubt that the Belgians were behind this move, ostensibly led by Moise Tshombe, but actively financed and supported by foreign interests. The Belgians immediately sent troops into Katanga to protect it from Lumumba's forces and supposedly to protect Belgian lives.

Under pressure from all sides, Lumumba became confused and accepted bad advice. Rather than seeking to negotiate and using the United Nations to resolve the crisis, he appealed to the Soviet Union for military support. His attempt to retake Katanga by force failed, and on 5 September President Joseph Kasavubu suddenly dismissed Lumumba as prime minister. Although the Congolese parliament voted to reinstate him, it was too late, for on 14 September Colonel Joseph Désiré Mobutu staged a military coup and took over the country, starting a long period of bloody dictatorship.

For a few weeks Lumumba was kept under house arrest, but his days were numbered. In Washington, President Eisenhower and the Central Intelligence Agency (CIA) had already decided to get rid of a leader who they saw as a trouble-maker. The CIA operations chief at the time later said, 'The President would have vastly preferred to have him taken care of some other way than by assassination, but he regarded Lumumba as I did and a lot of other people did: as a mad dog . . . and he wanted the problem dealt with.'

On January 1961, the 'problem' was dealt with, as Lumumba was assassinated in Elizabethville, Katanga. A few days earlier, he had written: "Neither brutality nor torture nor cruelty will ever bring me to ask for mercy for I prefer to die with my head unbowed, my faith unshakable, and with profound trust in the destiny of my country . . . Africa will write her own history and it will be a glorious and dignified history . . . Long live the Congo, long live Africa!"

So ended the brief and eventful life of Patrice Lumumba. We do not know whether he would have been a successful leader of a truly independent Congo, but we do know that he was one of Africa's great idealists.

DID YOU KNOW? So keen was the CIA to eliminate Lumumba that it sent a scientist to the Congo with a lethal virus to kill him. The virus was never used, as the CIA agent could not find anyone close enough to Lumumba to deploy it.

READ MORE: Robin McKown, *Lumumba: A Biography* (New York: Doubleday)

Malcolm X

1925-1965

During his short life, Malcolm X became one of the most influential and controversial spokesmen for militant Black Americans, becoming synonymous with Black Power and self-defence in the 1960s. His life was marked by violence and he was both a victim of and apologist for violent political action. He remains a cult figure among certain sectors of the Afro-American community, but during his lifetime he was feared and reviled by mainstream white opinion.

Malcolm X was born Malcolm Little on 19 May 1925 in Omaha, Nebraska. When he was still very young, his family moved to Lansing, Michigan. His father, Earl, was an outspoken supporter of Marcus Garvey and was an important influence on the young Malcolm. But holding such views carried real risks in the racist atmosphere of the Depression-era US, and in 1929, the Little family's house was burned down at night, apparently by the Ku Klux Klan. When the police and firemen arrived, they reportedly refused to help and watched as the house blazed. Later, Earl Little was arrested on charges of arson and for carrying a revolver without a licence. Worse was to happen two years later, when Earl was found dead, having been run over by a car.

Although the perpetrator was never discovered, Malcolm remained convinced that it was a racist murder. This was a turning-point in his life, and from then he became a rebellious child. Worn down by the financial hardships and emotional strains of bringing up eight children, Malcolm's mother was committed to the Kalamazoo psychiatric hospital when he was twelve. This marked the end of his family life and childhood.

Until he was sixteen, Malcolm lived with various foster parents (or in detention homes, according to some versions of his life story). Although he was a good and clever student, he was told that his dream of becoming a lawyer was unrealistic and he dropped out of high school early. Drifting from one dead end job to another, Malcolm moved to Boston, where he worked as a shoe shiner at a ballroom before arriving in New York six years later. It was here that he became involved with the criminal underworld in Harlem, reputedly making a living as a hustler and drug dealer. Not much is known about this phase in his life, but Malcolm was seemingly nicknamed 'Red' because of the colour of his hair. He managed to avoid being drafted into the military during the Second World War, but in 1946 he was

sentenced to eight years prison for burglary. After a year in Charlston Penitentiary, he was transferred to the experimental penal colony at Norfolk, Massachusetts.

This was the first piece of good luck in Malcolm's life, for it was here in a relatively relaxed prison atmosphere that he met a practising Black Muslim who persuaded him to read about religion and Black history. In the prison library he was able to obtain books by W.E.B. Dubois, the founder of the National Association for the Advancement of Colored People, as well as the works of such philosophers as Socrates. Inspired by this new education, he joined the prison debating team and competed against visiting students from Harvard.

On leaving jail, Malcolm was a changed individual. He joined the Nation of Islam (also known as the Black Muslims) and began working for the organization as somebody who could recruit other disenchanted Blacks. The Nation of Islam had been founded in 1930 and by 1952, when Malcolm joined, was led by the Honorable Elijah Muhammad. It taught its followers that they were the descendants of the Black inhabitants of Mecca and that they were destined to take over the world once white civilization had collapsed. In the meantime, the Black Muslims were commanded to have nothing to do with whites or non-Muslims and to develop their own society entirely separately. It was now that Malcolm Little became Malcolm X, in keeping with the Nation of Islam's rule that members had to get rid of the 'evil white name' given to their forefathers during slavery. Malcolm is also reported to have said that the new name was to remind the world that he was an 'ex-smoker, ex-drinker, ex-Christian and ex-slave'.

By the late 1950s Malcolm X was the best-known spokesman for the Black Muslims and had helped in setting up new mosques in Boston, Philadelphia and Hartford. In recognition of his appeal to young Blacks, Elijah Muhammad put him in charge of the mosque in Harlem, the most important in the US. Here Malcolm X worked as a minister, in touch with the poor youths in the inner city and much respected by many people in the community. His powers of oratory attracted large crowds to the mosque and to meetings, and his love of controversy and sense of humour made him a frequent guest on TV chat shows.

But Malcolm X's popularity and high profile were creating tensions with the movement's leader, Elijah Muhammad. There were also growing disagreements about political strategy, as Malcolm X was increasingly in favour of armed resistance to racist attacks and impatient with the Black Muslim policy of passive resistance. 'It doesn't mean that I advocate violence', he said, 'but at the same time, I am not against using violence in self-defence. I don't call it violence when it's self-defence, I call it intelligence.' He also had public disagreements with Martin Luther King, rejecting his teachings of non-violence and peaceful mass action. After the shooting by police of seven unarmed Muslims in Los Angeles in 1962, Malcolm X's attitude hardened further. The following year, when President John F. Kennedy was assassinated, he made his infamous remark about 'chickens coming home to roost'. By this he meant that the violence that was meted out to Blacks in the US had now come back to kill the President himself. There was widespread outrage that he seemed to be approving of the murder and Elijah Muhammad ordered him to be silent and suspended him from the Nation of Islam.

In 1964 Malcolm X left the Nation of Islam to form his own breakaway Black Muslim group, the Muslim Mosque, Inc. He warned white racists that he was now prepared to organize violence against them if necessary: '. . . if your present racist agitation against our people there in Alabama causes physical harm to Reverend King or any other Black Americans who are only attempting to enjoy their rights as free human beings, you and your Ku Klux Klan friends will be met with maximum physical retaliation from those of us who are not handcuffed by the disarming philosophy of non-violence and who believe in asserting our right of self-defence – by any means necessary.'

On a pilgrimage to Mecca the following year, he came to the conclusion that not all whites were evil (as he had seen white Muslims there) and modified his views. 'I have learnt that not all white people are racist', he said. He then formed another, more political grouping, the Organization of Afro-American Unity, with a strong civil rights agenda.

Malcolm X knew that his life was in danger, not just from the KKK and other extremists, but also from former allies. His house was fire-bombed, but nobody was injured. Then on 21 February 1965, he was about to speak on behalf of the Muslim Mosque, Inc in Harlem when he was shot and killed. Three members of the Nation of Islam were subsequently convicted of murder. 'He taught violence and he died violent', Elijah Muhammad is reported to have said.

Since his death, Malcolm X's reputation as a thinker and social activist has increased, thanks to the publication of his posthumous autobiography by Alex Haley and, more recently, Spike Lee's film about him. It is clear that if he had not died such an early and tragic death, he would have developed into one of the great Black leaders of 20th-century America.

DID YOU KNOW? After his pilgrimage to Mecca, Malcolm X changed his name once more – to El Hajj Malik Shabazz – in recognition of joining the universal Muslim brotherhood.

READ MORE: Alex Haley, *Autobiography of Malcolm X* (New York: Ballantine)

Nelson Mandela

1918-

Nelson Mandela will without question go down in history as one of the best-known and best-loved public figures of the twentieth century. As he had come to personify the heroic struggle against the evils of apartheid, he also symbolizes the qualities of forgiveness and reconciliation in the new nation of South Africa. His personal example as well as his political vision give him exceptional stature among his fellow South Africans – irrespective of race and colour – and in the entire the world, to whom he became a veritable icon.

Nelson Rolihlahla Mandela was born in the small village of Mvezo in the Transkei, on 18 July 1918. His father was a close friend and important associate of the then Regent of Thembuland and when he died, the young Mandela was adopted and brought up by the Regent. The Regent was the main legal arbiter in the region, and from him Mandela learnt from an early age the skills of leadership and governance

After primary and secondary education at local mission schools, he went to the University College of Fort Hare to read for a B.A. But there he soon became involved in politics, taking part in a protest boycott and being suspended from the College as a result. He then moved to Johannesburg, where he completed his degree by correspondence and continued studying to become a lawyer. It was at this stage, in the 1940's that Mandela joined the African National Congress (ANC).

Although the system of apartheid was not yet in force, South Africa was a deeply unequal country, with land, wealth and power firmly in the hands of the white minority. For thirty years the ANC had been a small organization, committed to non-violent opposition to white minority rule, but in the 1940s a new generation of activists resolved to turn it into a mass movement which would appeal to rural workers, shantytown inhabitants and professionals alike. Frustrated by the cautious conservatism of the ANC's old leadership, younger members set up the Youth League of the ANC, based on radical African nationalism. Together with Oliver Tambo, Mandela worked hard in the Youth League to win influence among the ANC membership and to introduce more hard-hitting policies. In 1950 Mandela was elected to the National Executive Committee of the ANC, on a programme that included full citizenship for all, direct parliamentary representation for all South Africans and redistribution of land. By 1952, he was busy travelling the country to organize a

massive civil disobedience campaign against the National Party government, which in 1948 had introduced its apartheid policy.

For his part in the Defiance Campaign Mandela was arrested and given a suspended prison sentence. He was also banned from attending political meetings and confined to Johannesburg. Using this period to finish his law studies and open a legal practice with Oliver Tambo, he began using his status as a lawyer to continue the fight for equal rights. By now, however, he was a particular target for government repression, and the authorities tried – unsuccessfully – to have him banned from practising as a lawyer. During this time Mandela also masterminded the celebrated M Plan, which organized ANC members into secret underground cells, capable of communicating among themselves without public meetings.

As Mandela became increasingly conspicuous as a leader of the ANC, he faced more and more harassment and repression. He was the number one accused in the notorious Treason Trial, which lasted for years, and was frequently arrested, imprisoned and banned from travelling. Finally, in the wake of the 1960 Sharpeville Massacre, in which sixty-seven Black demonstrators were killed, the ANC was banned and Mandela went underground. Moving from house to house, adopting different disguises, he became known as the Black Pimpernel. It was at this stage that he spearheaded the creation of armed nucleus of the ANC, Unkhonto we Sizwe (Spear of the Nation), ready to embark on an armed struggle against apartheid. This was not an easy move, for Mandela had long preached non-violence as the best strategy, but as he remarked: "It was only when all else had failed, when all channels of peaceful protest had been barred to us, that the decision was made to embark on violent forms of political struggle, and to form Unkhonto we Sizwe . . . The Government had left us no other choice."

Shortly afterwards, Mandela was arrested and charged with illegally leaving the country and incitement to strike. While serving a five-year sentence, he was also charged with sabotage and conspiracy to overthrow the government – much more serious offences. Instead of testifying at the historic Rivonia Trial, Mandela chose to make a speech from the dock; that speech had become a classic:

"I have fought against white domination, and I have fought against black domination. I have cherished the idea of a democratic and free society in which all persons live together in harmony and with equal opportunities. It is an ideal which I hope to live for and to achieve. But if needs be, it is an ideal for which I am prepared to die."

Mandela and his comrades were sentenced to life imprisonment and began their prison years in the notorious high-security Robben Island Prison, situated on a small island off the coast near Cape Town. For years they suffered a life of deprivation, kept apart from family, friends and direct involvement in South Africa's liberation struggle. But during that time, although he was behind bars, Mandela's symbolic stature continued to grow. All around the world, the slogan 'Free Nelson Mandela' became an intrinsic part of the campaign against apartheid. His controversial wife, Winnie Madikizela, kept Mandela's name in the headlines, while the ANC continued to grow in strength.

Eventually, the apartheid government was forced to acknowledgethat world opinion and on 11 February 1990 Mandela was released from the Victor Verster Prison, to where he had been moved in 1988. The scenes of celebration in South Africa and abroad were incredible, but Mandela maintained his dignity and his message of reconciliation. In 1991, at the first legal ANC conference for decades, he was elected party President and began the delicate job of negotiating an end to apartheid with President F.W. de Clerk. As the international community prepared to lift its sanctions against South Africa, the country readied itself for the first free and fair elections in its history.

Under Mandela's leadership, the ANC swept to power in the 1994 elections and he was inaugurated as President in May that year, at the age of 75. I went down to South Africa as part of the team sent to see that the elections were free and fair. Mandela immediately spoke out against his people seeking revenge and, in doing so, proved his leadership and statesmanship. Like other great Black leaders such as Jomo Kenyatta who have emerged 'from the prison to the palace', he did so without bitterness or desire for revenge.

In June 1999 the ANC won a second electoral victory and Mandela handed over power to his successor Thabo Mbeki. By no means all of South Africa's problems have been solved since his release, and there is still much poverty, crime and violence. But Mandela, honoured by the Nobel Peace Prize in 1993, has achieved a great victory in steering his country through a peaceful transition, ending in a multiracial democracy. This is what he dreamed of during the long years on Robben Island and this is what he will be remembered for by many generations to come.

DID YOU KNOW? When the South African government offered to set him free in the 1980s on condition that he renounced violence, Mandela declined to accept. Prisoners cannot enter into contracts, he said, only free men can negotiate.

READ MORE: Nelson Mandela, *Long Road to Freedom* (New York: Little, Brown)

Index